MODERN

PARLIa

MᵉNTARY

MODERN PARLIaMENTARY PROCEDURE

RAY E. KEESEY

AMERICAN PSYCHOLOGICAL ASSOCIATION

Washington, DC

First edition published 1971 by Houghton Mifflin. Revised edition published 1994 by the American Psychological Association.

Published by the
American Psychological Association
750 First Street, NE
Washington, DC 20002

Copies may be ordered from
APA Order Department
P.O. Box 2710
Hyattsville, MD 20784

In the United Kingdom and Europe, copies may be ordered from the
American Psychological Association
3 Henrietta Street
Covent Garden, London
WC2E 8LU England

Printer: McNaughton & Gunn, Inc., Saline, MI
Cover designer: Grafik Communications, Ltd., Alexandria, VA
Technical/production editor: Olin J. Nettles

Library of Congress Cataloging-in-Publication Data
Keesey, Ray E.
    Modern parliamentary procedure / Ray E. Keesey.
        p.   cm.
    Originally published: Boston : Houghton Mifflin, 1974.
    Includes bibliographical references and index.
    ISBN 1-55798-251-1. ... ISBN 1-55798-236-8 (pbk.) (acid-free paper)
        1. Parliamentary practice.   I. Title
    JF515.K395   1994
    060.4´2...dc20   94-11948
                                                                          CIP

British Library Cataloguing-in-Publication Data
A CIP record is available from the British Library.

Printed in the United States of America
First APA printing June 1994

To two friends,
whose encouragement prompted me to undertake
the simplification of parliamentary rules
for the conduct of meetings:
G. Bruce Dearing and John W. Shirley

Contents

11 Constitutions, Bylaws, and Rules 125

Note From the Publisher

Why would the publishing arm of a major scientific and professional association...and the American *Psychological* Association, at that...be reissuing a classic handbook of modern parliamentary procedure? What would prompt a publisher whose goal is the dissemination of theoretical, empirical, and applied knowledge in the discipline of psychology to add a book to its publication list that examines and propounds the fundamental principles and processes of orderly democratic deliberation? These are questions about which the bookseller, the potential buyer, and the reader may all legitimately inquire.

The answer is simple: Keesey's *Modern Parliamentary Procedure* has served our association eminently well since it was formally adopted for use by the extensive APA governing system in 1981. During this time, our boards and committees, ranging in size from perhaps half a dozen to as many as 135 Council members, have put the Keesey system to the test and discovered that the book is precisely what it claims to be: a practical, straightforward presentation of a simplified procedural system for open participation in and effective direction of deliberative meetings. As stated in an earlier foreword, Keesey's clarification of the system of motions and rules is "unfettered with exceptions and legalistic jargon." His book provides a singularly practical alternative to the few classic procedural texts, which are often viewed as more appropriate for use by the largest and most formalistic governing bodies.

If the reasoning and commitment to such a text is simple, the tale of how it came to be revised and reissued by an association publisher is somewhat more complex. The book was first released in 1974 by Houghton Mifflin Company. In 1984, a Barnes & Noble edition was issued. Since the late 1980s, however, the book has been largely unobtainable. So great was APA's interest in...and, indeed, reliance upon...the Keesey system that those involved in the governance of the association urged the publishing staff to seek out the author himself to explore the possibility of acquiring all rights to the publication and to the system. The process of locating the author was extended, and the search was often frustratingly derailed. Judy

Strassburger, of the APA Executive Staff office, cheerfully but determinedly insisted upon the value of the project and inspired flagging energies at several crucial points. Many individuals on the APA Books staff were involved in the search, particularly Julia Frank-McNeil, the Director of Acquisitions and Development, and W. Ralph Eubanks, the Director of Production. Susan Reynolds, the acquisitions editor, whose many hours on the telephone lines eventually put her in touch with Keesey's former secretary, Jane Harrington (who helped to prepare the original manuscript in 1971), must be especially acknowledged for her persistence. After two years—and with the help of a remarkable chain of personal assistance from U.S. Postal Service employees—we finally discovered that Mr. Keesey was retired, had moved to Florida, and had eventually relocated to Ohio. We established contact with him via his daughter, Mary Ann Scott, and finalized the details that resulted in the publication of the present edition.

Those familiar with previous editions will find this text largely unaltered. Some editing was done to enhance the originally tentative nonsexist approach to language, and an effort was made to update the footnotes and bibliography (we gratefully acknowledge the assistance of the APA Library staff in this latter task). In all other respects, however, the author's original aims, content, and language were scrupulously honored. Because we view it as a *living*...not a static... conceptualization, we intend to refine and further develop the Keesey system in future years, maintaining the author's original philosophy for an evolving, simplified-but-effective parliamentary system.

We believe that Keesey's *Modern Parliamentary Procedure* represents an equally indispensable tool for small club and organization boards as for larger association or corporate governance bodies. APA Books is pleased to place this book back into general circulation, and we recommend it heartily. Please send comments and suggestions to APA Books, Acquisitions and Development, 750 First Street, NE, Washington, DC 20002-4242.

Gary R. VandenBos, PhD
Washington, DC
May 1994

Foreword

Dr. Keesey's book, *Modern Parliamentary Procedure*, is a giant step toward the much needed modernization of parliamentary procedure and toward the better implementation of the fundamental principle that parliamentary procedure should facilitate the transaction of business in an orderly, deliberative democratic manner.

For decades there has been a serious need for a modern book on parliamentary procedure, one that would serve as a suitable, up-to-date parliamentary authority, a book acceptable to the vast number who dislike the misleading terminology and ill-advised complications of parliamentary orthodoxy. Dr. Keesey's book fulfills this need and improves parliamentary procedure so that it is easier for vital, controversial issues to be solved by parliamentary means rather than by violence or dictatorial action.

Modern Parliamentary Procedure presents numerous methods for more efficient democratic action. Its contributions include modernizing parliamentary terminology, presenting a simpler and more logical classification of motions, eliminating several troublesome, superfluous motions, and providing some valuable ideas concerning the prevention and handling of disruptions.

Robert W. English
Founder, American Institute of Parliamentarians

Preface

This book is a manual of simplified parliamentary procedure, entirely compatible with accepted parliamentary principles but free of the traditional mysterious jargon of the professional parliamentarian. This book's specific points of departure from other manuals of parliamentary procedure are

1. Reduction in the number of motions
2. Simplified precedence of motions
3. Elimination of the "seconding" of motions
4. Emphasis on the principle of majority rule

The procedure is truly simplified. The total number of motions is considerably reduced, and each motion says exactly what it means, requiring no restatement or translation by the presiding officer. Superfluous motions have been eliminated, and "subsidiary and privileged motions" have been combined into the single category, Ordinary Motions. Unnecessary and confusing motions have been relegated to Chapter 6, "Motions Not Recommended." Many distinctions in the rank of precedence of motions have been eliminated, and the student or group member will find less rote memory required for effective participation in meetings. Time will be saved by not insisting on the seconding of motions. In general, stressing a more straightforward and open procedure for meetings eliminates the parliamentary impasses that appear to follow when too much attention is given to parliamentary intrigue and manipulation. It is therefore easier to participate in a meeting conducted under the rules in *Modern Parliamentary Procedure,* and the authority for flexibility in administering rules rests firmly in the assembly itself. In this way, organizations using *Modern Parliamentary Procedure* will find their meetings more democratic in operation.

R. E. K.

Introduction

Winston Churchill is said to have remarked that legislative procedure is an enigma wrapped in a mystery. It should not be mysterious. For one thing, most people do not need to know all of its rules. In selecting rules for inclusion here, I have made a fresh beginning, taking nothing as sacrosanct. My operating principle has been to ask "What really is essential?" to a group considering a proposition. The result, I believe, makes the democratic principles of parliamentary procedure much more functional.

Progress in simplifying parliamentary rules has already been made by Hellman, by Sturgis, and by other recognized authorities.[1] Further simplification of the procedural rules is needed particularly by groups that operate without benefit of a parliamentarian.

I originally hoped to advocate fewer rules, perhaps in entirely new terminology. However, practical considerations, growing out of more than twenty years' experience as a parliamentarian and a continuing interest in the subject as student and teacher, argue against further simplification. Fairness in the handling of motions, the flexibility to modify motions before voting, and freedom to rectify mistakes after a vote has been taken must be assured by rules known to all.

---

1. Hugo Hellman, *Parliamentary Procedure* (New York: Macmillan, 1966); Alice Sturgis, *The Standard Code of Parliamentary Procedure*, 3rd ed. (New (New York: McGraw-Hill, 1988).

A Basic Parliamentary Approach

Groups need to know the rules only for those motions they normally use; most other specially required procedures may be formulated, and their limitations agreed to, by majority vote *at the time the need arises.* As any experienced parliamentarian knows, special situations do arise that call for procedures not covered specifically in any manual. The exercise of common sense by the presiding officer and parliamentarian, consistent with the basic principles of parliamentary procedure discussed in Chapter 1, should point the way to solutions. The assembly's approval of any special procedures should be invited by the presiding officer whenever feasible. This is discussed more fully in Chapter 7.

Simplified Rules and Terminology

The rules of parliamentary procedure tell how, when, and why to use motions. A *motion* is a form of expression, usually beginning with the familiar and time-honored words "I move that . . .," used to present ideas to a group for consideration.

What rules are essential? *Robert's Rules of Order Newly Revised* lists more than eighty motions. Busy members of voluntary organizations cannot be expected to memorize these, as well as the six or eight categories that apply to each motion.

In a few cases, rules have been simplified by allowing one motion to serve purposes that previously required separate motions. In other instances, actions previously undertaken only by means of formal motions may now be accomplished without the use of motions at all. Those who question the wisdom of omitting some of the traditional motions will find in Chapter 6 a list of those no longer recommended, with a brief explanation for the exclusion of each.

Legal Requirements for Procedure

A compelling reason for following acceptable procedure is the possibility of a court action brought by a person who feels that his interests have been slighted. Thousands of court cases in which the verdict turned on the validity of a decision-making procedure have been examined by Mason and Sturgis.[2] Mason defines *parliamentary law* as the rules and principles that the courts apply in judging a controversy growing out of the process of decision making.[3] The law presumes that deliberative groups will follow their own constitutions, bylaws, and rules and in all cases not covered by these will be governed by parliamentary law.

Court decisions have been handed down protecting the right of a minority to be heard, defining a majority vote, outlining the authority of tellers in handling secret ballots, forbidding the secretary to cast a unanimous ballot in elections, and defending the right to freedom of debate, among other issues. Members of an organization, as well as the presiding officer and parliamentarian, should understand the need to follow acceptable procedures. This is not meant to imply that any special procedures can assure that group decisions will be legal. As O'Brien points out, skill in the use of acceptable parliamentary procedure is more practicable than a broad knowledge of civil law and its relation to parliamentary procedure.[4]

---

2. Paul Mason, *Mason's Manual of Legislative Procedures* (New York: McGraw-Hill, 1953); Sturgis, *The Standard Code.*
3. Paul Mason, "The Law and Parliamentary Procedures," *Adult Leadership* 5 (December 1956): 188≈190. James W. Cleary, one of four original collaborators on *Robert's Rules of Order Newly Revised*, took the somewhat different position that rules of order are firmly based on the principles and practices of voluntary democratic organizations and do not depend for their validity on court decisions. See "A Commentary on Robert's Rules of Order Newly Revised," *Parliamentary Journal* 9 (April 1968): 3≈9. Since court decisions are largely based on precedent, it is advisable for any organization to avoid procedural practices that the courts have found invalid.
4. J. F. O'Brien, *Parliamentary Law for the Layman* (New York: Harper & Bros., 1952), p. 208

The Parliamentary Authority

A *parliamentary authority*, once adopted in an organization's bylaws, becomes the basic source of its procedural rules. A parliamentarian advising a presiding officer is expected to follow the adopted parliamentary authority, whether or not he would prefer another. Organizations that find *Modern Parliamentary Procedure* to their liking should amend their bylaws to adopt it as their parliamentary authority. Otherwise, the benefits of its innovations may not be available to them.

Designation of the Presiding Officer

The presiding officer has traditionally been called the chairman. The word *chairman* has been used for many years as a generic term applied to both sexes. More recently, however, the term *chairperson* has been chosen by many organizations as a more suitable generic designation. In practice, the presiding officer of most groups is the president, who, when presiding, may still be called president. *Presiding officer, president, moderator, the chair, chairman, chairwoman,* and *chairperson* are all appropriate designations depending upon the circumstances and the usage assigned by an organization in its bylaws. It should be up to individual groups to select and vary the use of these terms as they see fit.

Summary

A need exists for greater simplification of parliamentary procedure, despite previous efforts in this direction. Many organizations have adopted a parliamentary authority not generally understood by their members. A large portion of the most frequently adopted parliamentary authority is probably too complicated for most members of volunteer organizations, who cannot be expected to do the detailed study necessary to understand it. And much of it is unnecessary for such organizations.

Chapter 1

The Basic Principles

Description and Discussion

Majority Rule

As Thomas Jefferson put it, "The voice of the majority decides." This principle (*lex majoris partis*) is at the heart of democratic procedure. It is another way of saying that conflicts may be resolved by agreeing to accept a decision, solution, or recommendation approved by more than half of those voting. It assumes...and the principle is not workable otherwise...that those in the minority agree to accept the decision of the majority. Whether or not it is stated as a condition of membership, any member of an organization whose meetings are governed by parliamentary procedure agrees to abide by the mandate of the majority.

In a very real sense, the observation of parliamentary rules is the surest way to determine the opinion of the majority. Under no circumstances may a group suspend the *principle* of majority rule. It may adopt certain rules for its own use, such as a rule closing debate by a two-thirds vote, but in the absence of any special rule to the contrary, the majority of the eligible votes cast, assuming a quorum present, represents the will of the majority. By applying the principle of majority rule, any group may decide what it is willing to consider and what it is not willing to consider. It may postpone consideration until a more convenient time, or it may modify any pending proposal to make it represent the will of the majority. Finally, it may decide at any time to adjourn the meeting.

Although a quorum must be present for an organization to conduct business legally (except in those few circumstances listed on page 23), a quorum is usually no more than half the membership, and sometimes considerably less. Therefore, a legal majority may in fact be a majority of a minority, and the actual votes cast for the majority decision may represent a small fraction of the group's total membership, or even of a quorum.

The Rights of the Minority

During the decision-making process, the apparent minority has the right to be heard, to oppose what appears to be the majority's position, and to try to persuade others to accept its point of view. It is often not known until the vote is taken which position has the majority. Members voting with the minority retain all the rights and privileges of membership and may not be discriminated against because of their votes. They may not be forced to vote on any question. They have the same rights as any other members to propose a motion and to speak and vote for or against a motion.

While accepting the majority's decision, the minority member may continue to plan strategy intended eventually to make the minority's point of view that of the majority. For example, when a committee reports to its parent group, a minority report may be presented as an amendment to the committee report, and a vote taken on substituting the minority report for the committee report. This subject is discussed further under Committee Reports in Chapter 8.

Many parliamentary rules are intended specifically

to protect the rights of members of the minority. They may not be deprived of their rights to debate unless a vote to that effect (usually requiring two thirds) passes; they may expect that the agenda will be covered in the order specified in the call for the meeting (unless two-thirds vote to suspend the rules); they may not be deprived of the right to have their proposal considered (unless a majority votes to remove their motion from consideration); and they may assume that certain actions, such as amending a bylaw, will not be taken in a meeting unless they have received previous notice, as specified in the bylaws, that these actions are to be considered.

Equality of Members

Each member of a deliberative organization conducting its affairs in accordance with parliamentary procedure has the same rights, privileges, and duties as any other member. He or she has the right to present a proposition for consideration, to discuss and recommend it for adoption, and to have it critically examined by his or her colleagues before a vote is taken. He or she has a right to demand that the presiding officer put propositions above personalities and call on members as they request the floor, trying to balance the expression of pro and con arguments on a proposition, and not permitting a one-sided presentation.

All members have the right to be nominated for office and to have their election to office determined by secret ballot. They have a right to expect courteous treatment from others when they have the floor, and a duty to extend this courtesy to others. They have a right to expect that the parliamentary rules of an organization will be fairly administered, and they may not be denied the privileges of attending meetings and participating on an equal basis with all of the other members. They may expect that their vote will carry the same weight as that of any other member, and that they may, if they wish, refrain from voting.

Freedom of Discussion

The right to be heard and to hear what others have to say about a motion before voting on it is basic to intelligent group action. How one votes may well be determined by evidence, analysis, and persuasion presented during the discussion of a motion. Freedom of discussion is integral to other basic principles, including the rule of the majority, the rights of the minority, and equality of membership. No member may have the right to "speak his or her piece" circumscribed, except by rules that similarly limit the rights of all of the members. The motion to close debate is misused if it is offered to prevent members from stating their views. Since such a motion deprives a minority of freedom of debate, it requires a two-thirds vote to pass. Its use should be infrequent and is only justified to prevent repetition of argument when it is apparent that little is to be gained from further discussion. It may be used to deter a small but vocal minority from pressing its position to the point of exhausting and exasperating an apparent majority.

Other Principles

The rule of the majority, the rights of the minority, equality of membership, and freedom of discussion are the four most fundamental principles of democratic action. Parliamentary rules of procedure exist to ensure their observance. Mention should be made of some other principles perhaps less crucial but important for a more complete understanding of the need for certain parliamentary rules. Among them are

1. Only one main motion may be considered at any given time.

2. Members have a right to know at all times what the immediately pending motion is, and to have it restated before a vote is taken.

3. Organizations may take official action only in meetings properly called, and with a quorum of members present.

4. Actions taken by organizations are not valid if they tend to subvert either the civil laws of the nation, state, or local governmental unit or the rules of a parent organization.

The principles of parliamentary law may appear self-evident, or indistinguishable from those on which all democracies are based...as indeed they are. But it cannot be too heavily emphasized that blind adherence to parliamentary rules without an appreciation of their relation to democratic principles can only lead to a shallow conception of their real purpose. On the other hand, proper appreciation of these principles may result in an attitude toward administration of the rules that will guide a presiding officer or a member to wise and tolerant participation in group meetings.[1]

Some Groups Require More Rules Than Others

When a group is capable of decision making in an informal way, without the use of parliamentary rules, it should do so. This type of meeting usually requires a group small enough to permit considerable informality, and a patience and sophistication in human relations rarely shared by all the members. It is wrong to insist that all groups, regardless of size and also degree of internal harmony, hold to the letter of all parliamentary rules. O'Brien recommends that the degree of procedural formality be adapted to the group's unity, size, and knowledge of acceptable parliamentary procedure.[2]

In small groups, certainly including committee meetings, informal procedures are often preferable. The presiding officer should request a formal vote only when a decision must be made and unanimity seems impossible within the time available. In small informal groups, it

---

1. Giles W. Gray, "A Philosophy of Parliamentary Law," *Quarterly Journal of Speech* 27 (October 1941): 437≈441.
2. J. F. O'Brien, *Parliamentary Law for the Layman* (New York: Harper & Bros., 1952), p. xvii.

may be helpful to discuss the wording of a motion before actually proposing it, thereby avoiding the time-consuming process of amending the motion to reach the agreed form. In all such proceedings, the presiding officer may save time by using the informal procedure of general consent. That is, when group opinion appears to have crystallized, the presiding officer may announce, "If there is no objection, we will. . . ." Members, of course, must be ready to prevent abuse of this procedure; a single objection forces a vote.

Arguments for Limiting the Use of Parliamentary Procedure

Research in social psychology, problems of group development, and the dynamics of decision making have led some to feel that voting is less desirable than consensus as a means to decide questions. The Quakers have long been highly respected for their practice of taking "the sense of the meeting."[3]

Some have argued against using parliamentary procedure in decision making. One of the most common criticisms is that its use invites polarization within a group, the forces for a motion aligning against those opposed to it. Many decisions are arrived at only by the narrowest of margins, in a climate of *winning* and *losing*...not the best atmosphere for the enthusiastic and cooperative implementation of decisions. It also tends to discourage individuals from feeling a personal responsibility for decisions or for their fulfillment.

Other arguments could be marshaled in favor of approaching a problem-solving or decision-making situation without resorting to parliamentary rules. Such groups probably do, however, use a crude form of parliamentary procedure, and, of course, effectiveness is not assured by abandoning acceptable parliamentary procedure. It is possible that this point of view may mask

---

3. See Morris Llewellyn Cooke, "The Quaker Way Wins New Adherents," *The New York Times Magazine* 6 (June 17 1951): 21, 40≈42. Reprinted in *Parliamentary Journal* 5 (October 1965): 12≈18.

a failure to study the basic rules of procedure, and a resulting ignorance of the flexibility possible within good parliamentary practice.

When Parliamentary Procedure Is Required

There are valid arguments for suspending parliamentary procedure under some circumstances. Cooperative problem-solving groups with enough time available will usually discover within their ranks leaders who can guide them to wise decisions. But many groups cannot operate in this way. Time is limited; problems are pressing; action is required. In these cases, the needs of the group tend to make preferable a more formal method of proceeding, involving the observance of common-sense rules to ensure that all members have an equal opportunity to participate, that minorities are not ignored, that the rule of the majority prevails, and the like. When groups cannot unite on the issues before them, and especially when time is a factor...as it always is...parliamentary procedure appears to be the best solution.

Fortunately, when groups turn to more formal procedures, they need not improvise rules. The path is well marked. They have at their disposal basic principles that have stood the test of time. The rules of procedure may vary according to the type of group and may be suspended to meet a specific need or changed, if the group desires. But the principles do not vary, and may be neither suspended nor changed. The rules of parliamentary procedure exist to protect the observance of democratic principles. Differences of opinion on procedural matters may often be resolved by asking how to ensure that basic principles are not violated.

Chapter 2

A Historical Sketch of Parliamentary Procedure

The Classical Origins

The basic principles of parliamentary procedure appear to have been clearly defined and practiced as early as the fifth century BC in Athens.[1] The Bible describes the Council of Seventy chosen to assist Moses, and there are references to deliberative assemblies in the Hebrew commonwealth as far back as 1200 BC.

The assembly (*ecclesia*) of Athens met regularly, usually on a hill called the Pynx, to listen to their spokesmen speak from a rock platform called the *bema*. The speakers were often military leaders reporting on their campaigns, or political leaders such as Pericles or Demosthenes. The assembly had prepared agenda, was presided over by a chairman, listened to all those who wished to speak, passed motions to prevent or limit debate as needed, and

---

1. J. F. O'Brien, "Historical Development of Parliamentary Discussion," *The Thomas Jefferson Parliamentarian* 4 (November 1960): 3≈19, and 4 (May 1961): 1≈20. Reprinted in *Parliamentary Journal* in three parts in October 1966, January 1967, and April 1967. O'Brien's article, to which this chapter is indebted, should be read by those interested in further information.

voted...usually by a show of hands...on propositions before them.

The highest deliberative authority in the Roman republic was the Senate. Composed of magistrates, not popular representatives, this group observed great formality in dress, tradition, and procedure. Other assemblies of lesser rank existed, but the Roman Senate, because of distinguished leadership exercised by the most outstanding men of the time, became universally respected for its soundness of judgment and wise counsel. In its deliberations, clarity and brevity were applauded, and the "purple patches" of oratorical greatness of Cicero probably represented an exception to the general atmosphere.

The English Tradition

When the colonial congress of the United States was looking for procedure to govern its deliberations, it naturally turned to that used by the British Parliament. Parliamentary procedure in England had evolved through precedent from as early as the thirteenth century and was fairly well developed by the eighteenth century. A compilation of these rulings was published by John Hatsell, clerk of the House of Commons, in two volumes, one in 1776 and the second in 1781, and later reissued in four volumes. Referred to as *Hatsell's Precedents*, these volumes were the principal source of Thomas Jefferson's *Manual of Parliamentary Practice*, published in 1801. A written record of the proceedings of Parliament, often of doubtful authenticity, has been kept from 1509 for the House of Lords and from 1547 for the House of Commons. Not until 1908 did both Houses instigate an official recording of proceedings, no longer relying on private records.

Parliamentary Procedure in the United States

The development of parliamentary procedure in the United States after the adoption of the procedure followed in the British Parliament is best illustrated by a brief look at the three principal writers on the subject prior to the twentieth century: Jefferson, Cushing, and Robert.

Thomas Jefferson

Thomas Jefferson, as vice president and presiding officer of the United States Senate, recognized the need for a compilation of the rules of procedure, adapted largely from *Hatsell's Precedents*, he thought appropriate for Senate use. His *Manual of Parliamentary Practice*, published in 1801, the first year of his presidency, continues to be the principal parliamentary guide of the Senate and the House of Representatives, the latter having adopted it in 1837. Jefferson's *Manual* was the first significant publication on parliamentary procedure in the United States.

The extent of its influence was probably not anticipated by Jefferson, who wrote modestly of his own role as that of a "mere compiler" and did not consider the *Manual* worthy of inclusion in a proposed complete edition of his writings. His own original contribution he limited to the arrangement of the material and "a few observations" and examples.[2]

Luther S. Cushing

The second most significant publication on parliamentary procedure was by a Massachusetts lawyer and judge, Luther Stearns Cushing. Drawing on his experience as clerk of the Massachusetts House of Representatives from 1832 to 1834, Cushing wrote *A Manual of Parliamentary Practice; Rules of Proceedings and Debate in*

---

2. Letter to John W. Campbell dated September 3, 1809, in *The Writings of Thomas Jefferson*, edited by Paul Leicester Ford (New York: G.P. Putnam's Sons, 1898), vol. 9, p. 258. For more information on Jefferson's *Manual*, all in the *Parliamentary Journal*, see Richard S. Kain, "America's Parliamentary Inheritance from Thomas Jefferson," 7 (April 1966): 14≈18; Thais M. Plaisted, "Noted Legal Writers Quoted by Jefferson," 9 (January 1968): 13≈18; and "Historical Footnotes in Jefferson's *Manual*" 10 (January 1969): 3≈13.

Deliberative Assemblies. Published in 1845, it was generally known as *Cushing's Manual*. Considered more appropriate to the needs of nonlegislative groups than Jefferson's *Manual*, it was also widely used by legislative groups. Only four inches by six inches in its best-known form, *Cushing's Manual* sold extensively in the United States and abroad.[3]

Henry M. Robert

The most widely used book on parliamentary procedure today is that of Henry M. Robert. The *Pocket Manual of Rules of Order for Deliberative Assemblies* was first published in 1876. A new edition, titled *Robert's Rules of Order Newly Revised* (1990), has grown to over 700 pages, mostly because of an increase in the number of illustrations and examples.

Robert was an army engineer and a successful promoter of his manual, which is characterized by a degree of detail and an emphasis on parliamentary strategy regarded by some as more extensive than necessary. Robert apparently invented some rules to meet needs as he saw them. Some of his highly technical distinctions and lengthy observations appear unnecessarily complicated for the procedural requirements of many volunteer organizations today. Robert made a signal contribution, however, in calling the attention of thousands to the need for the study and practice of parliamentary procedure. He also attempted to standardize and to stabilize the rules of procedure for nonlegislative groups. In this his efforts were so successful that for many of his followers his rules became almost synonymous with parliamentary law itself. *Robert's Rules of Order* is today, however, and was from the beginning, only one system adapted to this purpose.

---

3. Cushing also published a longer, more legalistic work, Lex Parliamentaria, *Law and Practice of Legislative Assemblies*, in 1856.

Recent Guides

None of the guides to parliamentary procedure since *Robert's Rules of Order* has had as wide an acceptance as his. Some of the better known ones are by Auer, Davidson, Demeter, Hellman, Mason, O'Brien, and Sturgis. Of these the one by Alice Sturgis is probably best known. A few writers (Demeter, Mason, Sturgis) have gone to some lengths to show how court decisions and legal precedents stand as a basis for parliamentary rules. Others (O'Brien, Davidson) appear to accept the position that the rules are firmly grounded in the accepted practices of voluntary organizations and do not depend upon the sanction of the courts for their validity. Robert is a member of this latter group.

In addition to individual writers, many organizations have published parliamentary guides for their members. These include such large organizations as the American Medical Association, the Federated Women's Clubs, and Toastmasters International. These groups follow the practice that Robert himself found useful; when necessary, they invent or adapt rules to meet their particular needs. Any such special rules take precedence over those found in the adopted parliamentary authority.

Chapter 3

Introduction to the Rules of Procedure

Simplified Precedence of Motions

The term *precedence* refers to the rank of a motion in an established, or agreed-to, order for motions. Knowing the precedence for a motion, a member knows when the motion may be made and when it would be *out of order*.

Precedence of Ordinary Motions

1. To Adjourn
2. To Recess
3. To Close Debate
4. To Limit (Extend the Limits of) Debate
5. To Postpone
6. To Refer
7. To Amend

The motion To Adjourn has the highest rank or precedence. This means that To Adjourn is in order even though other motions are pending. On the other hand, a motion of low precedence, or rank, may not be made if one of higher rank is under consideration. For example, a motion To Amend is out of order if offered when To

Refer is pending; it would be in order only if nothing of higher rank than the main motion were under consideration. Similarly, To Recess is out of order while To Adjourn is pending, but To Recess would be in order if To Amend and To Postpone had both been moved and the latter (of higher rank than To Amend) was under consideration. A main motion has the lowest rank of all. Most of the seven ordinary motions exist to facilitate the efforts of an assembly to arrive at a decision on a main motion. Precedence or rank among motions prevents confusion. Memorizing the precedence of motions is less difficult when there are fewer kinds of motions involved.

Special Motions

> Point of Order
>
> To Appeal
>
> To Withdraw
>
> To Suspend the Rules
>
> To Reconsider
>
> To Rescind

Special motions have no rank in relation to each other, no necessary or predefined relationship. Except for To Reconsider and To Rescind, they exist largely to handle procedural matters that arise during the consideration of a main motion, and must be decided immediately.

A Point of Order is in order at any time, depending on its urgency, and may be followed by To Appeal. To Withdraw may be used at any time except to disrupt voting or to interrupt a speaker. To Suspend the Rules may be offered if a motion is pending, as may To Reconsider. All but Point of Order and To Withdraw are handled like any other main motion if moved when no main motion is pending. To Rescind is not in order if another main motion is under consideration.

Thus, in addition to the main motion, there are seven ordinary motions and six special motions. Only three of the thirteen require a two-thirds vote: To Limit (Extend the Limit of) Debate, To Close Debate, and To Suspend the Rules; all others need only a majority vote to pass. Most meetings will use only a few of the ordinary motions. In many meetings no special motions at all are introduced.

Any organization should feel free to modify the order of precedence when it appears desirable, either by general consent or by suspending the rules with a two-thirds vote. Thus, if a member moves to postpone the consideration of a question with a proposed amendment until a later meeting, and it appears wiser to refer the consideration to a committee, there is no reason why, by general consent, the motion To Refer to a committee may not be considered, even if To Postpone has been moved and stated by the chair. If To Refer is passed, the motion To Postpone is, of course, ignored and the main motion and its proposed amendment are sent to a committee for its recommendation. The point is that rules exist to serve the group, not the reverse.

Among the special motions, only To Suspend the Rules requires a two-thirds vote. A Point of Order (which is a request or a demand, not a motion), To Withdraw, and To Suspend the Rules are not debatable, and only one of the six, To Rescind, may be amended.

Seconding of Motions

Motions need not be seconded. The requirement of a second is largely a waste of time. What member is so destitute of friends that he or she cannot find one willing to second a motion? The traditional justification for requiring a second is that at least two members should support a motion to justify its consideration. In practice, presiding officers routinely drone "Do I hear a second?" after each motion proposed, regardless of its merit and obvious appropriateness, and many members volunteer a "second the motion" even before the presiding officer's request. Often members do not understand the relevance or desirability of a motion until pertinent information is revealed in discussion. There is nothing essentially *wrong* with the practice of seconding. It is simply unnecessary.

It approaches the ridiculous when the chairperson of a committee whose members are facing each other around a table requires that one member second another's motion. Time wasted on this ritual should be saved for more fruitful purposes.

If seconding is intended to prevent frivolous and unnecessary motions from being offered, it is an ineffective deterrent since there is no reason to assume that only one member is so inclined. Control of unnecessary motions is best exercised by the presiding officer, who should address a few simple questions to the mover of the motion as to his intent and purpose. The presiding officer should rule frivolous and dilatory motions out of order.

When a motion is made, the presiding officer, without asking for a second, should either state the motion or rule it out of order. This procedure will also eliminate the necessity of remembering which motions require a second and which do not.

In summary, with regard to seconding of motions,

1. The presiding officer normally states the motion without asking for a second.

2. Seconding of motions is eliminated in order to (a) avoid an unnecessary complication, (b) save time, (c) remove an unwise deterrent to the making of motions, and (d) lessen the temptation to debate a motion before making it.

Presence of a Quorum

A *quorum* is usually defined as the minimal number of members of a parliamentary body who are eligible to vote and who must be present in order to conduct business legally. The number constituting a quorum is defined in the bylaws; otherwise, common sense and common law usually define a quorum as a majority of the members of an organization. For a mass meeting that does not have the status of an organization, a quorum is the number present at the meeting.

It is the responsibility of the presiding officer to determine the presence of a quorum. He or she usually does this by checking quickly on the number of members present or by asking the secretary, parliamentarian, or another member to report on the status of a quorum. If the count is close, the presiding officer should announce the presence of a quorum as she or he opens the meeting, to reassure doubting members on this point. It is also the responsibility of the presiding officer to determine the presence of a quorum in the course of a meeting if there is reason to believe one no longer exists because members have left...the situation known as a "disappearing quorum." If a quorum is no longer present, the presiding officer must either close the meeting or limit the group to those actions permissible in the absence of a quorum. These actions are discussed below.

If a quorum is not present when it is time to begin the meeting, the presiding officer should wait a few minutes to see if more members arrive. If a quorum does not convene, and it is already ten or fifteen minutes past the scheduled opening time, the presiding officer should announce the absence of a quorum and state that, unless a quorum can be rounded up, any business transacted (with the few exceptions to be noted later) will be unofficial and invalid. He should firmly resist suggestions by members that they proceed with the agenda in the hope that a quorum may later appear.

Among the valid actions which may be taken by an organization in the absence of a quorum are to adjourn, to take a recess, to set a time for the next meeting, or to take action to secure a quorum. It may also hear committee reports (but take no action on them), listen to remarks by members and others, and take emergency action if necessary, in the hope that such action will be approved at a later meeting with a quorum present.

If there is no quorum at a required meeting, such as one scheduled in the bylaws, the absence of a quorum does not invalidate compliance with the rules. The meeting was held, quorum or no quorum, and need not be rescheduled to comply with the requirement of a legal meeting. The meeting is legal; the conduct of most business without a quorum is not.

Organizations tend to set quorums too high. A quorum should be no larger than the number of members that might normally be expected to attend regularly scheduled meetings. Varying seasonal attendance and transportation problems in unfavorable weather should both be taken into account. Members who attend a meeting at some personal sacrifice of time and money feel justifiably disappointed and frustrated at the absence of a quorum.

This vexing problem is not limited to voluntary organizations. The United States House of Representatives adjourned once in 1966 and once in 1968 for want of a quorum; the United States Senate adjourned once in 1968 for the same reason. In both the House and the Senate, members may appear in the chambers to answer to their names and be included in the quorum count, and then leave. After trying for two hours and fifteen minutes to get enough members to answer for a quorum, Senate Democratic leader Mike Mansfield adjourned the Senate on September 24, 1968 when he finally secured the fifty-first member for a quorum, to find that only fifteen Senators were actually present.

There is no universally applicable rule for determining the number for a quorum. Each organization must judge what is best for its particular situation. In an organization with actively interested members from a contiguous area, a quorum of one half of the members may present no problem. In an organization of similar size characterized by less active interest on the part of members and dull, sometimes unnecessary meetings, a quorum of ten percent may be too high.

Selecting the number for a quorum is a matter of good judgment. A quorum set too high may discourage attendance for fear a quorum may not convene, and one set too low may permit an unrepresentative minority to take advantage of the membership.

A quorum for a committee should usually be not less than one half the committee's membership. However, in a committee which takes no binding actions, simply recommending actions to the assembly, it may be wise to set the quorum at less than a majority, or even to specify that those present constitute a quorum. Organizations should state in their bylaws the requirements for a quorum, including that for standing committees; otherwise, a quorum is assumed to be a majority of the membership.

It should be emphasized that attendance at meetings, and therefore the presence of a quorum, varies with the content of meetings. Members cannot be expected to attend meetings that are perfunctory and lack interest. Unless there is a genuine need for a meeting, it should be canceled, with provisions for cancellation clearly outlined in the bylaws. On the other hand, the presiding officer and other officers should share the responsibility of adequate preparations for necessary meetings. The preparations should include the distribution in advance of a clearly worded agenda, including the names of any guest speakers; arrangements for visual presentations, if desirable; and advance provision of a good public address system and of comfortable lighting and ventilation in an area relatively free from disturbing noises.

To summarize, a quorum is essential for official business to be conducted, that is, for action to be taken on the meeting's agenda, with certain exceptions. It is the duty of the presiding officer to determine the presence of a quorum before opening the meeting. It is also the duty of any member, including the presiding officer, to question the presence of a quorum if he or she believes it is lacking, even if the meeting began with a quorum. The question of a "disappearing quorum" may be raised at any time, except to interrupt a speaker; a member rises and, without necessarily waiting for recognition from the presiding officer, states, "Mr. Chairperson, I question the presence of a quorum." The presiding officer must then determine if a quorum is present. If a quorum is obviously present, the presiding officer should consider repeated calls to determine the presence of a quorum dilatory, and hence out of order.

The question of the presence of a quorum must be raised immediately after a vote is taken for the absence of a quorum to invalidate that vote. "Immediately after" means prior to consideration of the next item on the agenda, or of any new subject, whether or not it is on the agenda. It is too late to invalidate an action after intervening business has been conducted, even if the absence of a quorum is then determined. The law presumes the continuing presence of a quorum if the meeting begins with one, and regards all actions taken as legal unless evidence clearly shows the absence of a quorum at the time of voting.

Chapter 4

Main and Ordinary Motions

The Main Motion

Definition and Purpose

A *main motion* is the statement of a request for action, an idea for evaluation, or the introduction of a *resolution* stating the group's position on a subject. It should be uncomplicated, as clear and concise as possible, and stated in the affirmative since the negative form is likely to result in confusion in voting. The presiding officer should request rephrasing of a motion if necessary to improve its clarity or may alternately suggest a rephrased version for the approval of the proposer.

Consideration of a main motion may be the reason a meeting is held. The principal business of the meeting may be to determine the opinion of the assembly on the motion and to translate this judgment, when necessary, into a formal commitment by the assembly.

Requirements (D, A, M, R)

A main motion is debatable (D); it may be amended (A); it almost always requires a majority vote (M) to pass; and the vote on it may be reconsidered (R). It is usually in order at any time there is no other main motion under consideration.

Forms and Examples

A main motion is usually a declarative statement introduced by the expression "I move that. . . ." For example,

- I move that we donate twenty dollars to the Red Cross.
- I move that we attend church this Sunday as a group.
- I move that we purchase the property on South Street.
- I move that we appoint a committee to investigate and to recommend the feasibility of our purchasing group insurance.

Discussion

A main motion may take the more ceremonious form of a resolution, presented in writing. In a resolution, a series of introductory clauses beginning "Whereas . . ." precede the action clause, which begins, "Now, therefore, be it resolved that. . . ." Once a resolution is presented and accepted for consideration by the assembly, it is handled just like any other main motion.

A main motion in the form of a resolution is often used to express an organization's formal position on an issue or to set forth an opinion in detail. It should be worked out carefully before the meeting, perhaps by several interested people willing to collaborate to find the right wording. It is a mistake to try to perfect the resolution under the pressure of an impatiently waiting assembly.

> Resolved that this association express its appreciation to the retiring secretary, Mrs. Helen Brown, for her long years of faithful and efficient service.

Longer, more formal resolutions, usually beginning with a preamble (a series of Whereas clauses), should take the following form:

Whereas, The . . . and,
Whereas, The . . . and,
Whereas, The . . ., therefore be it
Resolved, That . . ., and
Resolved, That. . . .

To prevent confusion, only one main motion may be considered at a time. While its usual form is as illustrated above, there are some special motions and some ordinary motions that are handled as main motions. These include

- To Reconsider a vote
- To Rescind a previous action
- To Amend a motion already adopted
- To Amend the bylaws
- To Appeal, if offered when no motion is pending
- To Recess, if offered when nothing else is pending or if qualified
- To Adjourn, if qualified, such as including a time for adjournment in the motion, or if adjournment is moved without providing for another meeting

These motions are discussed further in the appropriate sections below.

Summary

A main motion is debatable and amendable, and its consideration may be referred to a committee or postponed; it usually requires only a majority vote to pass; the vote on it may be reconsidered; and the action taken, under most circumstances, may later be rescinded. Resolutions are main motions, usually more formal in structure and presented in written form, which set forth a position or opinion.

Ordinary Motions

To Amend

Definition and Purpose. An amendment is a change in the wording of an amendable motion, usually a main motion, to make it express more accurately what the majority wants it to say, before it is voted on.

Requirements (D, A, M). To Amend is debatable (D), amendable (A), and requires a majority vote (M) to pass. The special meaning of "amendable" in this case is explained on page 31.

An amendment requires only a majority vote to pass, even if a two-thirds vote is required to pass the motion amended, as in the case of To Limit (Extend the Limits of) Debate, or To Amend a proposed change in the bylaws. When proposed on a debatable motion, amendments may have applied to them the motions To Limit or To Close Debate, and To Withdraw from consideration. A proposed amendment to a nondebatable motion, however, such as To Limit (Extend the Limits of) Debate, is not debatable.

A proposed amendment may not be separated from the motion it amends. Therefore, it may not *by itself* be referred to a committee, nor its consideration postponed to another time.

Forms and Examples. The exact change proposed, and its location in the motion, should be accurately specified. Some recommended forms follow:

- I move *to delete* all after "Tuesday morning" in the motion.
- I move to amend *by striking* the word "four" *and inserting* for it the word "six" in the motion.
- I move *to add* to the motion the words "at the discretion of the President."
- I move *to insert* the words "compact model" between the words "four" and "automobiles," making the passage read, if adopted, "the authorization for purchase of four *compact model* automobiles."
- I move to amend *by substituting* for the motion "that we donate twenty-five dollars to the Christmas Fund" the following motion; "that the Treasurer send a check for fifty dollars to the local welfare office to assist needy families at Christmas."

Discussion. The following ordinary motions may be amended:

- To Amend…if the change proposed is accepted without formal motion and vote.
- To Refer…as to size of committee, selection process, deadline for report, conditions of referral, etc.
- To Postpone…as to the limits of postponement.
- To Limit (Extend the Limits of) Debate…as to number of speakers, etc.
- To Recess…as to duration of recess.

The process of further modifying a proposed amendment to a main motion deserves special attention. Members must be free to effect as many changes in a motion as are required to make it state accurately the wishes of the assembly. The procedure for change should be easy for the average person to follow. For this reason, the confusing and redundant To Amend the Amendment is dropped as a parliamentary motion.

This does not mean that it is impossible to amend an amendment. It means either that suggested changes in a proposed amendment are accepted without a formal vote, or that the originally proposed amendment is voted on first and the suggested change to it is offered later as another proposed amendment. Thus, *only one proposed amendment is pending at a time.*

An experienced presiding officer will have little difficulty with this procedure. In most cases, a suggested change in a proposed amendment may be incorporated simply by the presiding officer's asking permission of the mover of the original amendment. If the suggested change is of questionable merit in the minds of some members, perhaps including the presiding officer, and unacceptable to the mover of the original amendment, the presiding officer may state, "After the proposed amendment is voted on, opportunities will be given to present other suggestions as separate amendments" and proceed with discussion of the pending amendment.

In brief, changes in a proposed amendment are

agreed to informally, or by general consent if requested by the presiding officer; if the proposed change is not accepted in this fashion, it can be offered later for separate consideration. In this limited sense, proposed amendments may be further amended.

This procedure eliminates the confusing term Amending the Amendment, a term that should not be used even in the informal consideration of a requested change. Instead, one should refer specifically to the proposed change; there is no need to label it.

This procedure is already used by hundreds of small groups under, say, forty members. And it should always be used by groups of only ten to fifteen and by committees. In meetings of large organizations, the presiding officer's skill in human relations may be challenged by this approach, but the overall simplification is well worth it. In practically all cases, it saves time otherwise required for formal consideration and vote on the "secondary amendment," as it has been called. Even if a suggested change in a proposed amendment is later put to a vote as a proposed amendment itself, this process does not make necessary any more votes than would have been required To Amend the Amendment. Of course, any number of proposed changes germane to an amendment may be accepted before putting the revised form to a vote.

A special form of amending called *Filling Blanks* is a timesaving device that may be used to resolve questions when several options are in need of consideration at the same time. This may involve deciding on an amount of money, a name, a preferred date or time, and the like, to be included in a proposed amendment to a motion. It can also be used, particularly in small groups, to secure group preference for one of several possible items or forms of wording for inclusion in the initial statement of a motion.

An example may help. Suppose a motion to send a delegate to the annual convention is under consideration, and the discussion centers on who would go if the motion were passed. Several names are mentioned. A blank might be created by amending the motion to delete the words "a delegate," with the understanding that the blank will be filled by vote. If four or five members are nominated, the group votes for or against each, in the order nominated, and the name of the person receiving the highest affirmative vote is entered to fill the blank. Discussion continues on the main motion.

This is a form of amending a motion. Of course, the motion discussed above could initially have been introduced with a blank to be filled by vote of the members. An alert presiding officer, seeing multiple choices presented that need consideration in changing a motion, may suggest, "If there is no objection, the choice will be determined after the manner of filling blanks."

Amendments proposed to a main motion should be germane...that is, closely related...and appropriate to the motion to warrant consideration. An amendment should not be used to change an affirmative proposal of action into a negative proposal *not* to take that action. An amendment should not be at odds with the general intent of the main motion, although it may be hostile to the proposed method of fulfilling the intent of the main motion.

It is sometimes difficult for the presiding officer to decide whether or not to accept a proposed amendment. When in doubt, the presiding officer is advised to ask the assembly if there is objection to considering the proposal as an amendment. If a member objects, a vote should be taken. A majority vote in favor of consideration would be required. Because this decision would be made by the assembly, no appeal could be entertained on it. No amount of effort at defining what is germane can take the place of common sense on the part of the presiding officer and the assembly in determining whether a proposed amendment should be considered.

In the case of a *substitute motion*...that is, a motion replacing the main motion...proposed as an amendment, the procedure outlined above is followed. If entertained as germane, informal changes in the amendment are permitted; if the vote on the substitute amendment carries, the original main motion is replaced by it, and the new main motion may be further amended before a vote is taken to approve or reject it.[1]

When a main motion with a proposed amendment pending is referred to a committee, the proposed amendment remains attached. It is considered again when the motion is reintroduced to the assembly, perhaps with a committee's recommendation on the wisdom of adopting the proposed amendment. The same course is followed when To Postpone the consideration of a main motion and its proposed amendment is passed by an assembly.

To amend a motion previously passed is a main motion, and is handled like any other main motion. It is debatable, amendable, and requires a majority vote to pass. However, no motion previously passed may be amended by a lesser vote than was required to pass the main motion originally. Thus, a motion that required a two-thirds vote to pass may not be amended by less than a two-thirds vote.

Access to a main motion previously voted on is also possible via the motion To Reconsider, provided the vote was taken in the same session. A proposed amendment to a bylaw is a main motion. It usually requires previous notice of intent to amend and a two-thirds vote to pass, depending on the provisions included in the bylaws.

Summary. A main motion may be amended as many times as the assembly wishes, but only one proposed amendment may be considered at a time. A proposed amendment may be modified by general agreement, or

---

1. This eliminates a complicated procedure that permits a substitute motion to be entertained as a *primary* amendment, and a second substitute called a *secondary* amendment considered on first the original motion and then to the substitute motion, before voting on the substitute motion. And when a committee reports on a motion…one that had proposed primary and secondary amendments pending when it was referred to the committee…by recommending a substitute motion for the original main motion, the situation invites confusion. The terms *primary* and *secondary* relating to amendments are used in *Robert's Rules of Order Newly Revised,* 9th ed. (Glenview, Ill.: ScottForesman, 1990). On page 130, Robert states that he prefers these terms over saying "amendments of the first [second] degree," although all are accurate designations.

by consent of the mover of the proposed amendment, as many times as the group wishes before putting it to a vote.

To Refer

Definition and Purpose. The motion To Refer is almost always used to send the consideration of a main motion to a committee. The most frequent use of To Refer is to permit a smaller group of selected, more knowledgeable members to give a motion detailed consideration and to report their findings back to the parent group. To refer a motion to a hostile committee in order to kill it is not a legitimate use of referral.

Requirements (D, A, M). The motion to refer to a committee is debatable (D) and may be amended (A) as to the number on the committee, the selection process, instructions to the committee, the deadline, and instructions for reporting. It often saves time to include this information in the wording of the original motion To Refer. Referral to a standing committee need not include this information, since it has probably already been written into the bylaws. The motion To Refer requires a majority vote (M) to pass. The vote on a motion To Refer may not be reconsidered, since the motion may be renewed in the same meeting.

Forms and Examples. The simplest form of a motion To Refer is as follows:

I move we refer this motion to a committee.

It is preferable to state the motion as follows:

I move we refer the consideration of the motion that [stating the motion] to a committee of three, appointed by the chair, to report at our next meeting.

Discussion. Chapter 8 discusses the functions of a committee, the selection of and duties of members, procedure in meetings, committee reports, and so forth.

Summary. The motion To Refer is debatable; it may be amended or withdrawn; it requires a majority vote; and it is in order if a proposed amendment is pending, but not if other motions ranking above it are pending (except by Suspending the Rules). If the motion fails, it may be renewed after further discussion, and debate on it may be limited or closed to expedite a decision. To Refer to a committee a subject not pending, or to appoint a committee to do a particular task not under consideration as a motion, is a main motion, treated like any other main motion.

To Postpone

Definition and Purpose. The motion To Postpone, if passed, removes a subject from consideration until the time or meeting specified in the motion To Postpone. Its purpose may be to set aside temporarily the consideration of a motion to permit consideration of more pressing business; to delay consideration and action until a more appropriate time; or to allow time for the development of a consensus or for caucusing, and so forth.

Requirements (D, A, M). To Postpone is debatable (D); may be amended (A) as to the time or conditions of postponement; and requires a majority vote (M) to pass. It applies to main motions only. It may have applied to it motions To Limit (Extend the Limits of) Debate, To Close Debate, or To Withdraw. A vote on the ordinary motion To Postpone may not be reconsidered, since the motion may be renewed in the same meeting.

Forms and Examples

- I move To Postpone this motion for fifteen minutes to permit the assembly to greet Senator Williams, who has just arrived.

- I move To Postpone until our next regular meeting the consideration of the motion that we purchase a station wagon for our organization.

- I move To Postpone consideration of the pending main motion until we have heard the quarterly report from the Committee on Finances.

Discussion. When one speaks of postponing a motion, it is technically, of course, the *consideration of the motion* that is postponed, not the motion itself. If the consideration of a motion is postponed until another meeting, the secretary lists it under "Unfinished Business" on the *agenda* for that meeting. To Postpone consideration of a motion until meaningful action is impossible, in order to kill the motion, is not a proper use of the motion To Postpone. A motion To Postpone consideration by referring to a committee is stated by the presiding officer as a motion To Refer to a committee, not To Postpone.

When postponement is suggested to permit consideration of a more pressing matter, or to deal with an emergency situation such as the unexpected arrival of a dignitary, the motion should specify that the pending business be postponed until the other matter has been resolved. The motion thus postponed is returned to consideration at the appropriate time by the presiding officer, who states the motion and declares that it is again open for discussion, under exactly the same conditions as before it was postponed. Used in this fashion, the motion To Postpone includes the function of the obsolete motion To Lay on the Table, discussed in Chapter 6.

Summary. To Postpone ranks above the motions To Amend and To Refer. Thus, if a motion To Amend or To Refer is pending, the motion To Postpone is in order, but neither of these motions is in order if a motion To Postpone is pending (except by Suspending the Rules). To Postpone is not in order if motions of higher rank...To Limit (Extend the Limits of) Debate, To Close Debate, To Recess, and To Adjourn...are pending (except by Suspending the Rules). Proposed amendments to the main motion are postponed if consideration of the main motion is postponed. A motion To Refer is ignored if pending when a motion To Postpone is passed.

To Limit (Extend the Limits of) Debate

Definition and Purpose. The purpose of this motion is to permit an assembly to control discussion of a motion by setting limits on the time allowable for discussion before voting on the pending motion.

Requirements (A, 2/3). To Limit (Extend the Limits of) Debate, in either of its forms, is not debatable. It is amendable (A), as to the specific time limits involved, but these proposed amendments are not themselves debatable. Since To Limit Debate may infringe on the basic principle of freedom of discussion, a two-thirds vote (2/3) is required to pass. The vote may not be reconsidered, since the motion may be renewed in the same meeting. It is in order when any debatable motion is pending, but not, of course, when To Recess or To Adjourn is pending. Limitations on debate imposed by passing the motion To Limit Debate are not valid beyond the meeting or convention in which they were authorized. The effect of To Limit (Extend the Limits of) Debate ceases to apply when a motion is referred or postponed.

Forms and Examples

- I move To Limit Debate on the motion that [stating the motion] to no more than thirty minutes.
- I move To Extend the Limits of Debate to one hour to permit more thorough discussion of this motion.
- I move To Limit Debate to three speakers for each side of the question, each to speak no longer than five minutes.

Discussion. Motions To Limit Debate are implemented by the presiding officer, who announces when the limit has been exhausted and proceeds to call for a vote on the immediately pending motion. If a group has decided to limit debate on a main motion to, say, thirty minutes, such other motions as To Refer and To Postpone may be made during this thirty-minute period; if one of these other motions should pass, the motion to limit debate is invalidated. During the thirty-minute period, the assembly may also vote To Recess (the recess is not counted against the thirty minutes) or To Adjourn, ending the limit on debate.

Summary. Motions To Limit Debate or To Extend the Limits of Debate may be amended only as to the specific time limit or number of speakers involved. Proposed amendments are not debatable. Neither form admits debate, and both require a two-thirds vote to pass. The motion To Limit Debate is in order when any debatable motion is pending, and yields only to the ordinary motions To Recess and To Adjourn. To Limit (Extend the Limits of) Debate and To Close Debate are the only ordinary motions requiring a two-thirds vote, because they potentially curb a member's freedom of discussion.

To Close Debate

Definition and Purpose. When a motion To Close Debate is passed, all discussion on the pending motion (or motions) is terminated, and the assembly proceeds to vote on the immediately pending motion, unless a motion of higher rank, such as To Adjourn, intervenes.

Requirements (2/3). To Close Debate is not debatable and requires a two-thirds vote (2/3) to pass. It is not amendable in the usual sense, but, by general consent, its form may be changed to make it applicable not only to the immediately pending motion but also to other pending debatable motions, or vice versa. Its consideration may not be postponed or referred to a committee, and a vote on it may not be reconsidered. Like all motions, it may, of course, be withdrawn from consideration before voting. It may not be applied to undebatable motions.[2]

Its usual form is "To Close Debate on [stating the pending motion]." It may be applied to any main motion and to the ordinary motions To Amend, To Refer, and To Postpone, as well as to the debatable special motions To Appeal, To Reconsider, and To Rescind. When so moved

---

2. In what appears to be an unnecessarily complicated device, *Robert's Rules of Order Newly Revised* (pp. 195-206) permits the motion To Close Debate (The Previous Question) to be applied to the undebatable motions To Limit (Extend the Limits of) Debate and To Recess for the purpose of preventing amendments to these amendable motions.

and carried by a two-thirds vote, its effect is to bring to an immediate vote the motion on which it was moved. After that vote has been taken, its effect has been exhausted.

Another form of the motion, however, is permissible. A member may move "To Close Debate on all pending motions." If, for example, a main motion, a motion To Amend, and a motion To Postpone were pending, a favorable vote To Close Debate on all pending motions would require votes on all three motions, starting with the last motion made. That is, the assembly would vote first on To Postpone consideration of the main motion, then on the motion To Amend the main motion, and finally on the main motion itself, perhaps as amended. If the first vote passes, of course, consideration of the main motion and the proposed amendment would be postponed and the effect of closure of debate would be exhausted. If the vote on To Postpone were negative, the assembly would proceed to vote on the proposed amendment and, regardless of the outcome of that vote, go on directly to vote on the main motion. Further motions To Amend, To Refer, and To Postpone may not be presented while the motion To Close Debate is still in effect.

Forms and Examples

- I move To Close Debate (understood to apply only to the immediately pending motion).
- I move To Close Debate on all pending debatable motions (applicable to the main motion, a proposed amendment, To Refer, and To Postpone, depending on what is pending when To Close Debate is moved).
- I move To Close Debate on the motions, To Postpone, and To Refer (that is, not to include the proposed amendment and the main motion within the scope of To Close Debate).

Discussion. The motion To Close Debate should be used infrequently. Too frequent use of this motion may reflect unfavorably on the presiding officer's skill in handling a group, or it may be symptomatic of factional dissension within a group or of attempted misuse of parliamentary strategy to prohibit information unfavorable to the motion from being revealed. It should not be entertained by the presiding officer (whose decision may be appealed and reversed) if a fair opportunity to discuss the motion has not been given to all interested members.

For two or three members to speak for or against a motion and then move To Close Debate is a travesty of parliamentary procedure if members who have not yet been heard are trying to present their views. Of course, it is out of order for a member to move To Close Debate at the conclusion of his or her own remarks or to include it in a motion he or she presents for consideration. However, when a small group insists on prolonging debate, perhaps intentionally delaying a vote by talking beyond the scheduled time for adjournment...that is *filibustering*...To Close Debate allows two-thirds of those voting to stop such dilatory tactics and bring the pending motion to a vote.

Summary. A motion To Close Debate may be applied to any debatable motion. It may be applicable to the immediately pending motion only or to some or all pending debatable motions. When passed in the latter form, it prevents motions To Postpone, To Refer, or To Amend from being offered and requires that votes be taken on all motions to which To Close Debate is applicable. If a motion To Refer or To Postpone is pending when debate is ordered closed on all pending motions, an affirmative vote on either To Refer or To Postpone removes the main motion from immediate consideration and cancels further application to it of the motion To Close Debate. This does not apply, however, when consideration of a motion is postponed only temporarily and resumed later in the same meeting. In this case, the effect of the motion To Close Debate remains applicable to the main motion when consideration is resumed.

To Recess

Definition and Purpose. To Recess is a motion to interrupt a meeting. Its purpose is often to provide a brief rest period in a tiring session, to continue a meeting to another day, or to break for a specific purpose (count ballots, refreshments), while also stipulating a definite time to reconvene the meeting.

Requirements (A, M). To Recess is not debatable; it may be amended (A) as to the time limit of the recess, and it requires a majority vote (M) to pass. Although the motion is not debatable, the mover of the motion To Recess, or of a proposed amendment to it, should be permitted to state his or her reason for offering the motion or amendment.

To Recess is in order provided the motion To Adjourn is not pending, since To Recess ranks above other ordinary motions and is outranked only by the motion To Adjourn. Proposed amendments to the motion To Recess are not debatable, and they must be limited in subject to the length of time of the recess or the specific times when it is to begin and end. A vote on the ordinary motion To Recess may not be reconsidered, since the motion may be offered again in the same meeting.

Forms and Examples

- I move we recess for ten minutes.
- I move we recess until the speaker arrives.
- I move we recess until ten o'clock in the morning (applicable in a convention, for example, at which the session consists of a series of meetings, and the motion To Recess, if passed, does not adjourn the convention).
- I move we recess until the ballots have been canvassed.
- (By the presiding officer.) If there is no objection, we shall recess for refreshments, reconvening at 10:45 A.M. (If there is no objection, the recess begins immediately.)

Discussion. A recess begins immediately on passing the motion To Recess. If a recess is announced in official agenda or a program, the presiding officer declares the recess in effect when the announced time arrives, and reconvenes the assembly at the expiration of the recess. No motions are required to effect these actions.

If made when there is no main motion pending, or if it provides for a recess to be taken at a later time, To Recess is a main motion, handled like any other main motion. When offered while a main motion is under consideration, however, To Recess ranks just below To Adjourn and is not debatable.

The motion To Recess must stipulate the duration of the recess, and thus provide for reconvening the meeting. There is no limit on the length of a recess, as long as it neither extends beyond the time set for the next regular or special meeting nor constitutes an adjournment, as in a convention. The motion To Recess is in order as a main motion in the absence of a quorum and may be used to await the presence of a quorum.

Summary. To Recess provides for an interval in the meeting, not an adjournment. It may be conveniently used when waiting for a speaker to arrive, ballots to be canvassed, or the room to be ventilated, or for a coffee break or brief cooling-off period in a heated discussion, and so forth. Little difficulty is normally encountered by the motion To Recess. To Recess may have applied to it only the motions To Amend and To Withdraw. When the presiding officer calls the meeting to order following a recess, the group resumes its considerations at the point at which it was interrupted.

To Adjourn

Definition and Purpose. Adjournment is the termination of a meeting or convention session, with the next meeting to be held following a new call for a meeting. When offered and passed in any but the last of a series of meetings in a convention, it should be recorded as a motion To Recess, not To Adjourn, since only the termination of the last meeting in a convention is, technically, an adjournment.

Requirements (M). To Adjourn is the highest-ranking ordinary motion. When not qualified in any way, and when made while a main motion is under consideration, it is neither debatable nor amendable and requires a majority vote to pass. It is in order at any time after a meeting has convened, provided the mover has been recognized by the presiding officer and does not interrupt a speaker or interfere with the taking or counting of a vote. It would not be in order if a motion To Adjourn had just been defeated and no intervening business had been introduced.

A vote on the ordinary motion To Adjourn may not be reconsidered, since it may be renewed in the same meeting after any intervening business has been introduced. To Adjourn is in order as a main motion in the absence of a quorum.

Forms and Examples

- I move that we adjourn. (When other business is pending, this is a nondebatable, nonamendable motion requiring a majority vote to pass.)

- I move that we adjourn until April 17 at 4:00 P.M. (If the time specified is that scheduled for the next regular meeting, this form merely constitutes a reminder, and the motion is limited as in the previous example.)

- I move that we adjourn until April 17 at 4:00 P.M. (If the time specified represents a previously unscheduled meeting, the motion is a main motion, in order only if no other main motion is pending, debatable, and amendable.)

- (By the presiding officer, when a time for adjournment has been previously fixed by an adopted rule, program, or motion.) The time set for adjournment has arrived. The chair is willing to entertain a motion To Adjourn.

  or

  Since our fixed time for adjournment has arrived, if there is no objection, the meeting is adjourned.

Discussion. To Adjourn is the highest-ranking ordinary motion. Under normal circumstances, nothing can prevent a majority of an assembly from terminating a meeting. If the agenda for a meeting has been completed and no one wants the floor, the presiding officer should adjourn the meeting by announcing, "Since there is no further business, if there is no objection, the meeting is adjourned." This is a legitimate procedure, implying a vote by general consent. No meeting is legally adjourned until the presiding officer *announces* the adjournment following a vote on the motion, whether counted or by general consent.

The presiding officer should not put the motion To Adjourn to a vote before making such necessary announcements as the time and place of the next meeting. In fact, in between taking a vote on To Adjourn and announcing the results of the vote, the presiding officer may give this information. If business must be considered after the presiding officer has entertained a motion To Adjourn, he may request permission to withdraw the motion, or, having explained the urgency of the situation, may state, "The chair requests that this urgent matter be attended to before adjournment" and proceed to state the question.

A motion To Adjourn to an Adjourned Meeting...that is, to continue a meeting at another set time...should be handled as is a motion To Recess; this eliminates the confusing terminology of that motion. The limitations imposed on the motion To Recess would, of course, apply.

What happens to the unfinished business of an organization when it adjourns? In an organization whose meetings are scheduled quarterly, monthly, or weekly, items on the agenda not covered before adjournment are carried forward to the next meeting as unfinished business. In organizations whose scheduled meetings are less frequent, all items on the agenda not covered when the meeting is adjourned are dropped. If they are included in the agenda for the next meeting, they are not listed as unfinished business.

When a meeting is continued to a time not representing a regularly scheduled meeting to permit the agenda to be covered, the motion To Recess is appropriate; the agenda is resumed at the exact point at which it was interrupted by the motion To Recess. An example is the prolonged consideration of extensive changes in a group's bylaws. Several meetings may be required, with perhaps as little as a day or a week between meetings, to complete consideration of the proposed amendments. In such successive meetings, the group should begin where it left off at the previous meeting.

Summary. To Adjourn, when unqualified, is the highest-ranking ordinary motion; it is neither debatable nor amendable and requires a majority vote to pass. When it is qualified in any way, it is handled like any other main motion. Official adjournment takes place only when the presiding officer announces the results of a majority affirmative vote, counted or by general consent, on the motion To Adjourn.

Chapter 5

Special Motions

Point of Order

Definition and Purpose

A Point of Order is the procedure followed to call the attention of the presiding officer to a violation of the rules, an omission or a mistake in the proceedings, or any unusual situation requiring immediate attention. Its purpose is to provide a means for a member to secure a ruling from the chair on a matter thought to be of sufficient importance to require immediate attention.

Requirements

A Point of Order is not debatable, not amendable, and requires no vote since the presiding officer decides the point at issue. It is in order at any time. The presiding officer should decide on the basis of its urgency whether it requires immediate action. One may interrupt a speaker to raise a Point of Order. That a Point of Order is not debatable should not prevent the member who raises it from explaining his or her position or the presiding officer from stating his or her position in ruling on the request.

Forms and Examples

1.   Member: Madam Chairwoman, I rise to a Point of Order.

      Chair: State your point.

      Member: We have two main motions on the floor.

      Chair: Your point is well taken. We shall consider only [stating the motion] at this time.

                 or

                 The only main motion now under consideration is [stating the motion]. Therefore, your point is not well taken.

2.   Member: I rise to a Point of Order.

      Chair: State your point.

      Member: We can't hear the speaker.

      Chair: Will the speaker please speak up so he can be heard?

3.   Member: Mr. President, I rise to a Point of Order.

      Chair: State your point.

      Member: I resent the insulting language of the speaker and his insinuations about the motives of members who support the motion.

      Chair: Your point is well taken. The speaker will please be more temperate in his language and will please confine his discussion to the merits of the proposal and not question the integrity of members.

Discussion

A member may appeal the ruling of the presiding officer to the assembly, following the procedure outlined in the next section. On the other hand, if the presiding officer is in doubt about the proper response to a Point of Order, he may refer the decision to the assembly for a decision by majority vote. There is no appeal from a decision of the assembly on a Point of Order.

A Point of Order is not a motion at all, but the protected privilege of a member to call the presiding officer's attention to something. Technically, a Point of Order is raised to inform the presiding officer of an infraction of the rules and to demand that proper procedure be followed, when further delay would only compound the error. It is sometimes used, however, for requests unrelated to infractions of the rules: A member may rise to a Point of Order to state that the room is too hot or that the speaker can't be heard, or simply to ask a question regarding proper parliamentary procedure. Such requests may properly be considered points of order if the implied rights of members are being violated. For example, a member has the right to have reasonable provision made for his or her comfort and to hear what is being said. These requests are not technically Points of Order, but they can be handled as such by the presiding officer in less time than it takes to explain the minor procedural variation involved, and the presiding officer should do so. The abuse of such requests is, of course, harmful, but rules alone cannot prevent it.

The Point of Order may be used in any of the following circumstances:

- To question the validity of the parliamentary procedure being followed (as in Example 1 above).

- To call a speaker to order for the inappropriate use of language or another breach of decorum (as in Example 3).

- To call attention to a condition that inconveniences members (as in Example 2).

- To raise a parliamentary inquiry, or to call attention to a violation of correct procedure.

- To question a ruling by the presiding officer on a point of parliamentary procedure prior to appealing his decision to the judgment of the assembly.

Summary

A Point of Order should only be used for urgent situations. It is a method of drawing the immediate attention of the presiding officer and the assembly to a pressing problem. If a member has overestimated the urgency of her or his Point of Order, the chairperson may state that she or he will answer it later when to do so would not interrupt a speaker. A ruling on the part of the presiding officer may be appealed by any member to the judgment of the assembly. Appeals may not be made on points involving the correctness of procedures since their accuracy may be checked by consulting the rules. The presiding officer's opinion about a rule does not constitute a ruling.

To Appeal

Definition and Purpose

To Appeal the ruling of the presiding officer means to subject his or her ruling to examination by the assembly and to secure its support or reversal. The purpose of this motion is to monitor the appropriateness and accuracy of the presiding officer's rulings and to prevent the arbitrary exercise of power.

Requirements (D, M)

To Appeal is debatable (D) and may not be amended, postponed, or referred to a committee.

To be in order, an appeal must be raised immediately after the ruling in question is made by the presiding officer; the mover may interrupt a speaker to do so. It may have applied to it the motions To Limit (Extend the Limits of) Debate, To Close Debate, and To Withdraw.

In putting an appeal to a vote, the question is always stated in such a way that the affirmative vote to support the ruling of the chair is requested first, followed by the negative vote to reverse the ruling by the chair. A majority vote (M) in the negative is required to overrule the ruling of the presiding officer; a tie vote sustains the ruling of the presiding officer.

If made when a main motion is not pending, the

appeal becomes a main motion and is treated accordingly.

Forms and Examples

1. Member: Ms. President, I appeal from the ruling of the chair that [stating the decision].

   Chair: The ruling of the chair that [stating the decision in question] has been appealed from. Will the member please state his reasons for appealing?

   Member: [States his reasons.]

   Chair: [States reasons supporting his ruling.] Is there other discussion on the motion? Are you ready to vote?

   Chair: Those in favor of accepting the ruling of the chair that [stating the ruling] please hold up their right hands. Thank you. Those opposed, the same sign. Thank you. The ruling of the chair is upheld by a vote of 21 to 9.

   or

   The ruling of the chair is reversed by a vote of 10 in favor and 14 opposed, and the judgment of the assembly is that [stating the decision of the assembly].

2. Member: Mr. Chairperson, I rise to a Point of Order.

   Chair: Please state your point.

   Member: We have erred in permitting amendments to the motion To Limit Debate. This motion may not be amended.

   Chair: Your point is not well taken. To Limit Debate is amendable as to time limitations, and the amendments permitted were of this type.

   Member: Mr. Chairperson, I appeal from the ruling of the chair.

   Chair: Since this is not a ruling by the chair, no appeal can be entertained. Our adopted parliamentary authority, *Modern Parlia-*

mentary Procedure, states on page 38 [reading the requirements for the motion To Limit Debate].

3.   Member: Madam President, I appeal the ruling of the chair made earlier in this meeting that my proposed amendment to the motion [stating the motion] was not germane.

        Chair: Mr. Speaker, that main motion has been disposed of. Therefore, your appeal is out of order. To be in order, a motion To Appeal must be offered immediately after the ruling in question is made by the chair.

Discussion

When a member wants to determine whether the presiding officer's ruling is consistent with the wishes of the assembly, he or she may appeal from the ruling of the chair. This procedure is often undertaken in response to the presiding officer's ruling on a Point of Order.

Care should be taken to appeal only *rulings* by the presiding officer. Appeals may not be made on accepted truths, known facts, existing laws, or established rules. That a main motion is debatable, for example, is not subject to appeal. The announcement of a vote or the answer to an inquiry on parliamentary procedure may not be appealed, since verification by other means is readily available. Any ruling involving the presiding officer's personal judgment or opinion, however, is subject to appeal, including such issues as whether or not a proposed amendment is germane or what constitutes misconduct on the part of members.

Summary

An appeal permits any member to submit his or her doubts about the validity of a ruling by the chair to examination by the assembly. Since the appeal must be proposed immediately following the ruling in question, a member may interrupt a speaker to request an appeal. The appeal must be decided immediately on being requested.

To Withdraw

Definition and Purpose

To Withdraw a motion is to remove it from consideration. The purpose of To Withdraw is to provide a means for terminating consideration of a motion without actually voting on it. It permits abandonment of a motion whose consideration might prove embarrassing to the assembly. To Withdraw has been widened in scope to subsume the purpose and function of the motion To Postpone Indefinitely, discussed further in Chapter 6.

Requirements (M)

To Withdraw is not debatable, although the mover should be permitted to state his or her reasons. It is not amendable and requires a majority vote (M) to pass. A request To Withdraw a motion may, however, be granted by the chair without a vote, regardless of the stage of consideration the motion has reached. If there is objection, a vote may be taken "that the motion [stating the motion] be withdrawn." Any motion may be withdrawn; no other motion may be applied to the motion To Withdraw.

Forms and Examples

1. Member: Mr. President, I request permission To Withdraw my motion that [stating the motion].

    Chair: The motion that [stating the motion] is withdrawn.

2. Member: Ms. Chairwoman, I move that the motion that [stating the motion] be withdrawn from consideration.

Chair: Please state your reasons for requesting the withdrawal of the motion.

Member: A discussion of this motion will require revelation of the personal finances of some members of this organization and will be embarrassing to them.

Chair: Very well, if there is no objection. . . .

Member: I object, Ms. Chairwoman. The motion should be considered even if some members must give personal financial information.

Chair: There has been objection to withdrawing the motion. Those in favor of withdrawing the motion that [stating the motion] please raise your right hands. Thank you. Those opposed to withdrawing? Thank you. The motion To Withdraw has passed by a vote of 27 to 11, and the motion that [stating the motion] is withdrawn.

3. Member: Mr. Chairman, I request permission To Withdraw my motion that [stating the motion].

Chair: There is obvious interest in the motion, as evidenced by our discussion of the motion for the past thirty minutes. Please state your reasons for wanting To Withdraw it.

Member: I had no idea that some members felt so strongly on this motion, and I would like To Withdraw it to prevent further antagonisms from developing.

Chair: Very well, if there is no objection, the motion will be withdrawn.

Member: Mr. Chairman, I object to withdrawal of the motion.

Chair: There has been an objection to withdrawal of the motion. The motion is to grant the member permission to withdraw his motion. Those in favor of granting such permission, etc.

Discussion

Before a motion has been stated by the presiding officer, the mover may withdraw it by stating, "I withdraw my motion." A motion may be withdrawn either by request of the mover or by a formal motion To Withdraw by any member at any time previous to the final vote on the motion. Withdrawal of a motion may be granted by the chairman, by general consent, or by a majority vote of the assembly. The effect of granting the withdrawal of a motion is the same as if the motion had never been proposed. Therefore, a withdrawn motion may be renewed, if appropriate, in the same or later meetings.

A motion that has been withdrawn after having been stated by the presiding officer is recorded by the secretary with a statement that it was withdrawn. The secretary does not record a withdrawn motion if it is withdrawn before being stated by the presiding officer.

Summary

The motion To Withdraw provides an assembly with a means to eliminate a motion without revealing how members stand on it. The motion may take the form of a request To Withdraw by the mover of a motion, or that of the more formal proposal by any member, "I move that the motion [stating the motion] be withdrawn."

To Suspend the Rules

Definition and Purpose

To Suspend the Rules is to set aside or make inoperative in a given situation a rule of order that would otherwise prevent the assembly from taking a desired action. Its purpose is to allow an organization to violate its own rules of procedure when the circumstances warrant.

Requirements (2/3)

To Suspend the Rules is not debatable, not amendable, and requires a two-thirds vote (2/3) to pass; the vote on it may not be reconsidered. When approved, it sets aside *temporarily* a rule of order to permit a particular action to be undertaken, and its effect expires when that action is completed.

Forms and Examples

1. Member: Madam Chairperson, I move To Suspend the Rules to hear the report of the Special Committee on Convention Planning before the regular standing committee reports.

   Chair: If there is no objection [pausing] the rules will be suspended to permit the report of the Special Committee on Convention Planning to be heard now. Will the chairperson of that committee please proceed with the committee report?

2. Member: Mr. President: I move To Suspend the Rules to consider items under Unfinished Business immediately.

   Chair: If there is no objection, we will go immediately to the first item under Unfinished Business on the agenda.

   Member: Mr. President, I object.

   Chair: There has been objection to the motion To Suspend the Rules. A two-thirds vote in favor of Suspending the Rules is required to change our rules of order governing the order of business. Those in favor of Suspending the Rules to permit taking up items under Unfinished Business immediately, please raise your right hands, etc.

3. Member: Madam President, I move we Suspend the Rule requiring a quorum so that we can get down to work.

   Chair: The rule stating that the presence of a quorum is necessary to conduct business legally may not be suspended. Therefore, the motion is out of order.

Discussion

Only procedural rules may be suspended. These may be either rules of order and standing rules or procedural rules set forth in the adopted parliamentary authority. The distinction between rules of order and standing rules is discussed in Chapter 11. To Suspend the Rules does not apply to bylaws. To avoid confusion on this point, organizations should list rules of order and standing rules separately from bylaws.

Certain rules may not be suspended. Members may not be deprived of their rights by suspending the rules. Rules governing voting methods and requirements, stipulating advance notice of a meeting, governing the conditions for calling a meeting, or setting a quorum may not be suspended. Although bylaws may not be suspended, if a rule of order is listed with the bylaws instead of separately, its location does not prevent its suspension by a two-thirds vote. The adopted parliamentary authority may not be suspended, although it may be changed by amending the bylaws.

On occasion, an organization may wish to proceed in its deliberations in a way that violates its own rules of order or standing rules. For example, suppose that debate on a motion has been closed by the usual two-thirds vote, when the assembly suddenly becomes aware that the only real expert among the members on the issue in question has just arrived. By suspending the rule prohibiting debate on a motion when it has been ordered closed, the member may be heard. As soon as he or she has finished, however, the effect of the suspension of rules expires. In this instance, the presiding officer would probably request general consent to suspend the rule in question and, if there were no objection, call on the member to speak.

To Suspend the Rules is in order when a motion is pending, if its purpose is related to that motion. Suppose that during the reports of standing committees, the presiding officer of a special committee finds that she must leave the meeting before she would be called on to report in the normal order of business. For her to present her report early would violate a rule of order governing the order of business. She or any other member may move To Suspend the Rule requiring her report to be given in accordance with the order of business and "to permit the report to be heard now." If passed, the rule is suspended only for the duration of the report in question; procedure then reverts to the accepted order of business.

Summary

To Suspend the Rules is used infrequently, but occasions arise when it is needed as an orderly and acceptable way of accomplishing a specific purpose. The vote on the motion To Suspend the Rules may be by general consent; if no one objects, the presiding officer announces that the rule in question has been set aside temporarily and proceeds to the matter now eligible to be brought to the attention of the assembly.

To Reconsider

Definition and Purpose

To Reconsider is to call back for further consideration by the assembly an action previously taken on a main motion. Its purpose is to permit a vote taken on a main motion *in the same meeting, session, or convention* to be set aside, and the motion again considered and voted on as if no previous vote had been taken on it.

Requirements (D, M)

To Reconsider is debatable (D), not amendable, and requires a majority vote (M) to pass. It may be withdrawn. It may not be moved on the same motion twice, and a vote on the motion To Reconsider may not itself be reconsidered. Its consideration may not be referred to a committee or postponed, but motions To Limit (Extend the Limits of) Debate, To Close Debate, and To Withdraw may be applied to it. The motion To Reconsider may be made while another main motion is pending, but its consideration is delayed until there is no other main motion pending. It may be applied only to votes on main motions, since other motions that have failed may be renewed after intervening business, and other motions that have passed may be changed by other procedural motions. For example, a passed motion To Refer may be changed by recalling from the committee the referred motion, and a passed motion To Postpone may be changed by a motion to resume consideration of the postponed motion.

Forms and Examples

1. Member: Mr. Chairperson, I move To Reconsider the vote on the motion that we contribute $100 toward the political campaign of Governor Wilson.

   Chair: A motion To Reconsider the vote on the motion that we contribute $100 toward the campaign of Governor Wilson is before you for discussion. Since no part of the $100 has been contributed and no other official action has been taken under the motion, the vote on the motion may be reconsidered. The floor is open for discussion on the motion.

2. Member: Ms. President, I move To Reconsider the vote on the motion that we attend church this Sunday as a group.

   Chair: A motion To Reconsider the vote on the motion that we attend church this Sunday as a group is before you for consideration. [Discussion.] Those in favor of reconsidering the vote on the motion that we attend church this Sunday as a group, please say Aye. Those opposed, please say No. [Vote.] The motion To Reconsider has passed and the motion that we attend church this Sunday as a group is again before us, just as it was before we voted on it. Is there discussion?

or

The motion To Reconsider has not passed. We shall continue with the next item on the agenda.

3. Member: Mr. Chairman, I move To Reconsider the vote on the motion that we hire an architect to plan the enlargement of our clubhouse.

   Chair: It is noted that a motion To Reconsider the vote on [stating the motion] has been made. We shall return to this motion To Reconsider following the disposition of the main motion now before us. Let us continue with our discussion of the main motion.

Discussion

This infrequently used motion permits an assembly to reexamine an action taken earlier that it subsequently finds questionable. It is in order only during the meeting, session, or convention in which the vote to be reconsidered was taken. Unwise actions discovered after a meeting closes may usually be corrected by the motion To Rescind, discussed in the next section.

The motion To Reconsider may be made by any member[1] and may be applied to affirmative or negative votes on main motions, but not to votes on motions that may be renewed within a reasonable time, such as To Amend, To Refer, and To Postpone, or to votes which have already resulted in irreversible action.

If the meeting, session, or convention is adjourned… not just recessed…before the motion To Reconsider is

---

1. *Robert's Rules of Order Newly Revised*, 9th ed. (Glenview, Ill.: ScottForesman, 1990], p. 77, among others, requires that reconsideration be moved by a member who voted on the prevailing side of the motion in question. Alice Sturgis (*The Standard Code of Parliamentary Procedure*, 3rd ed. [New York: McGraw-Hill, 1988], p. 35) points out the inappropriateness of this requirement.

taken up, it is as if the motion had never been presented. If made when nothing else is pending, the motion To Reconsider is handled immediately.

An alert presiding officer should not permit abuse of the motion To Reconsider. A motion to reconsider a vote immediately after the vote is taken, intended to prevent a later motion To Reconsider (since a vote may not be reconsidered a second time), should not be tolerated; nor should its use *ad nauseam* by a disgruntled minority to waste time and heckle the majority.

Summary

To Reconsider permits an assembly to correct an action taken under a misapprehension or with inadequate information. The vote on any main motion, whether passed or lost, may be reconsidered at the same meeting, session, or convention in which it was acted on. No vote on a main motion may be reconsidered, however, if some irreversible action has been taken on it, such as a payment of money, signing of a contract, or notification of an appointment and acceptance by the party concerned.

To Rescind

Definition and Purpose

To Rescind is to nullify a decision or action that cannot be changed by the motion To Reconsider. Its purpose is to cancel, or make void, the results of a motion previously passed.

Requirements (D, A, M)

To Rescind is a main motion, in order only when no other main motion is pending. It is debatable (D), may be amended (A) (*only* as to the portion of the decision to be rescinded), and requires a majority vote (M) to pass. It may be applied to main motions and to votes on appeals from the decision of the presiding officer. To Rescind opens to debate the main motion that it is intended to nullify. To Rescind may have applied to it the motions To Amend, To Refer, To Postpone, To Limit (Extend the Limits of) Debate, To Close Debate, and To Withdraw.

Forms and Examples

1. Member: Ms. Chairperson, I move To Rescind the decision taken at our last meeting that our convention be held in Boston.

    Chair: A motion To Rescind the decision taken in the last meeting that our convention be held in Boston is before you for discussion.

     If passed, the chair states,

     The motion To Rescind the decision taken in the last meeting that our convention be held in Boston has passed. Therefore, that action no longer stands. The next item on the agenda is. . . .

2. Member: Mr. President, I move To Rescind the motion passed last fall that this faculty award an honorary doctorate of laws to Mr. Marshall at our June graduation.

    Chair: The motion To Rescind the action of last fall awarding an honorary degree to Mr. Marshall is before you for discussion.

    Member: Mr. President, I question entertaining the motion To Rescind this motion since certain actions have been taken that may not be undone.

    Chair: Please explain your position.

    Member: Extensive publicity has already been given the faculty decision, and the proposed recipient of the degree has been notified of the action and agreed to be present to receive it. Therefore, I believe it is not possible To Rescind and the motion is out of order.

| Chair: | The chair stands corrected. The member is right, and the motion To Rescind is out of order. |

Discussion

It makes no difference how long ago the main motion to be rescinded was passed. Motions may not be rescinded, however, if irreversible actions have already been taken on them. For example, if money has already been paid for legal services, the action authorizing payment may not be rescinded. Or, if a person has been elected to membership, has been officially notified, and has accepted, the action may not be rescinded. However, unexecuted portions of a motion may be rescinded.

If a passed motion is rescinded, the minutes should record the passage of a motion To Rescind and also a statement of the motion, or the portion of a motion, rescinded.

To prevent fluctuations in attendance from permitting a smaller group to reverse a decision of a larger group, advance notice of the motion To Rescind may be required for a majority vote to pass; a two-thirds vote may be required to pass if no advance notice is given. Such a requirement may be adopted as a rule of order; but in the absence of such stipulations, a majority vote prevails. The vote required To Rescind, however, should never be lower than the vote that was necessary to pass the motion in question. That is, a two-thirds vote is necessary To Rescind a motion that required a two-thirds vote to pass.

Summary

The motion To Rescind, although seldom used, permits an assembly to rectify mistakes made in haste, to take into account new developments, or to invalidate motions passed by an unrepresentative minority in a poorly attended meeting. Any main motion or portion of a motion passed by an assembly may be rescinded, provided that irreversible action has not been taken on it.

Chapter 6

Motions Not Recommended

The thesis of this work is that parliamentary procedure may be simplified and still make all the necessary provisions for an organization to conduct its business. This is accomplished by eliminating several motions, still included in most other manuals, that almost invariably result in confusion. The functions served by these motions either are considered unnecessary or are fulfilled by other ordinary or special motions that are more easily used and understood.

Some of these motions have nonsensical names, such as To Lay on the Table, To Postpone Indefinitely, or The Previous Question. Others are so complicated that few members of groups feel competent to invoke them, such as To Object to the Consideration and To Reconsider and Have It Entered on the Minutes. Some are so infrequently used that they have never been heard in thousands of organizations, such as To Fix the Time to Which to Adjourn, To Make a General or a Special Order, To Call for the Orders of the Day, To Refer to a Committee of the Whole, and To Expunge From the Record. Others are used...and sometimes overused...when simpler and clearer methods for accomplishing the same purposes exist, such as To Raise a Question of Privilege, To Rise to a Parliamentary Inquiry, To Amend the Amendment, and To Close Nominations. Explanations of the decisions to eliminate these motions, and to simplify procedure generally, will be found in the following discussions of individual motions.

To Postpone Indefinitely

To Postpone Indefinitely, a motion whose name contradicts itself, is to reject a main motion without requiring members to vote on it directly. Two purposes of the motion are to take a *straw vote* to determine the strength of the opposing side, and to dispose of a motion undeserving of consideration without recording a vote on the motion itself. Small wonder that many have advocated dropping To Postpone Indefinitely! Complicated rules of gamesmanship are not needed in serious group deliberations.

The motion To Withdraw is available to get rid of unsatisfactory motions. It may be offered at any time and means just what it says, in both of its principal forms: when invoked by the original mover of a motion, it is a Request to Withdraw, usually granted routinely by general consent; when offered by a member other than the mover of the motion to be withdrawn, it is a motion That [stating the motion] be Withdrawn, and may be passed by general consent, or by majority vote. As a way of removing a motion from consideration, To Withdraw eliminates the confusion built into using To Postpone Indefinitely.

To Amend the Amendment

To Amend the Amendment may not trouble students of parliamentary procedure, but it has long been a source of confusion and frustration for those who have not made a special study of procedural rules. The terminology is inherently confusing. Skillful and experienced presiding officers are hard-pressed to state clearly the parliamentary situation when more than one proposed amendment is pending. Only one amendment, the last one stated by the presiding officer, is immediately pending but it is unlikely that all members understand why *three votes* are required to approve a main motion, a motion To Amend, and a motion To Amend the Amendment.

The function served by the motion To Amend the Amendment must be preserved, while its ambiguity and the difficulty of stating and handling the motion are simplified. There is no need to use the term To Amend the Amendment. Changes in a proposed amendment may be accepted informally, as they usually are in small groups, or by general consent. If there is an objection to accepting a change in a proposed amendment, a vote may be taken on the proposed amendment with the understanding that the suggested change may subsequently be proposed as a separate amendment. (This procedure is discussed more fully under To Amend in Chapter 4.)

To Refer to a Committee of the Whole, To Consider as if in a Committee of the Whole

The artificiality of a group referring the consideration of a motion to itself, under the pretense that functioning as a single large committee will allow it to proceed more effectively in its deliberations, approaches the ridiculous. And when the group later moves To Rise and Report to itself, in order to shed its playacting role as a committee and resume normal status, the ludicrousness of the situation is undeniable. Perhaps that is why these motions are never used in most organizations. A group may vote to allow itself any degree of informality in procedure, including a recess for the utmost freedom in consideration, without resorting to the subterfuge of these motions.

To Lay on the Table, To Table

Two good reasons for dropping this motion are that it does not mean what it says and that its intended use has been generally abused. The consideration of a motion is never literally laid on the table, or tabled. In the interest of accuracy and simplification, the names of motions should reveal their purposes. The purpose of this motion…to put aside temporarily the consideration of a motion…is well served by the motions To Postpone and To Recess.

To Table is now generally used, in the Congress of the United States and elsewhere, to kill a motion…another instance of the misleading use of language. Because the motion is undebatable, members may vote on it without ever learning why the mover wants the consideration tabled, unless reasons are stated in his motion To Table. Perhaps that is why many members often abstain from voting on a motion To Table, and a relatively small group of organized opponents of a motion may constitute the majority voting To Table or kill it.

If one's intent is to kill a motion, the motion To Withdraw should be used and the reasons for withdrawal explained openly and honestly; if the intent is to postpone consideration, the motion of that name is self-explanatory.

The Previous Question

The Previous Question is currently used to close debate when further deliberation is no longer profitable or desirable. This function is served by the motion To Close Debate, whose name means just what it says. Therefore, To Move the Previous Question, or To Call for the Previous Question, both incongruent expressions that usually require translation, should be eliminated. Their continued use cannot be defended on any ground other than loyalty to historical precedent.

To Fix the Time to Which to Adjourn

There is no need for this awkwardly stated motion, which is almost never used outside of instructional meetings in parliamentary procedure. A motion To Adjourn is debatable and amendable as a main motion if its effect would be to adjourn without providing for another meeting… that is, to disband the organization. If it is necessary to set a time for the next meeting, the motion To Recess until [stating the date and time] meets this need.

To Raise Question of Privilege, To Rise to a Parliamentary Inquiry

These are not motions, but procedures for making an individual request for action or information on procedure. These stereotyped forms are not needed to accomplish the purposes intended. In urgent situations involving the safety or comfort of members, any member should be privileged to ask the presiding officer to effect a remedy immediately, without having to resort to these forms. The degree of urgency should determine whether a speaker may be interrupted; if the presiding officer believes immediate action is required, he may even recess the assembly.

Many organizations do not differentiate between these two procedures and the Point of Order, considering all individual inquiries as Points of Order. Though this is not the use originally intended for a Point of Order, it is less confusing to allow a Point of Order to subsume these forms, since in all such cases the presiding officer decides on the validity of the request.

The Point of Order is the most logical refuge for these two obsolete forms (as well as for To Rise to a Point of Personal Privilege and To Request Leave to Ask a Question) since it allows members to appeal the decision of the chair, as discussed in Chapter 5. Use of the Point of Order to include all these functions is recommended with the understanding that the presiding officer must control the use of a Point of Order, subject to appeal by the assembly.

To Object to the Consideration

This is another unnecessarily complicated motion that cannot be put to a vote in the same language in which it is presented. Members and presiding officers of organizations cannot be blamed for steering clear of a motion that is not debatable, not amendable, requires a "two-thirds negative vote to sustain the objection," and is in order only immediately after the motion to which it applies has been stated by the chair.

If a reason for objecting to the consideration becomes apparent during the discussion of a motion, it is too late to object to its consideration; but it is not too late, of course, to request that it be withdrawn. The principal purpose of the motion is to prevent irrelevant, frivolous, or embarrassing motions from being considered. These the presiding officer should rule out of order anyway, either on his own initiative or by an affirmative ruling on a Point of Order requesting that the proposed motion be ruled out of order. If the ruling of the chair is reversed by an appeal, the motion must be considered. This procedure bypasses the awkward two-thirds negative vote to sustain the objection, and permits a majority vote...the vote appealing the chair's decision...to decide what may or may not be considered.

Mason[1] allows the Objection to the Consideration, though infrequently used, to be decided by a majority vote in legislative groups. Sturgis,[2] although noting the shortcomings of this motion, follows Robert in requiring a two-thirds vote, on the grounds that every member has a right to have his or her motion considered. But Sturgis and Robert provide for the presiding officer either to initiate the Objection to the Consideration and put it to a vote, requiring a two-thirds negative vote to prevent consideration, or to rule the motion out of order. If an appeal follows that is lost by majority vote, the ruling of the chair is reversed and the question is considered. In the first instance, a two-thirds negative vote is required to prevent consideration; in the second instance, a majority vote in the negative overrides the presiding officer's decision to rule the motion out of order and thus assures consideration.

It scarcely seems necessary to require a two-thirds vote to prevent consideration of a motion that, if consid-

1. Paul Mason, *Mason's Manual of Legislative Procedure* (New York: McGraw-Hill Book Company, 1953), p. 222.
2. Alice Sturgis, *The Standard Code of Parliamentary Procedure*, 3rd ed. (New York: McGraw-Hill, 1988), p. 223

ered, would be decided by a majority vote. The basic principle of majority rule should be sufficient protection of the right of members to present motions for consideration. Furthermore, since the presiding officer should rule out of order all motions she or he deems frivolous and unnecessary, the question of consideration is decided by a majority vote if the ruling that the motion is out of order is appealed.

If the presiding officer is in doubt whether a motion is in order, he or she should proceed by inviting the assembly to decide whether a proposed amendment is germane. That is, the presiding officer should say, "The chair is in doubt as to whether or not the proposed amendment is in order. Those in favor of considering the amendment. . . ." If a majority favors consideration, it is as if the presiding officer had ruled the amendment out of order and had the ruling appealed and reversed by a majority vote in the negative.

In the interest of simplification of the rules, the Objection to the Consideration should be eliminated. Its continued use is not recommended. If during the debate on a motion, legitimate reasons become apparent to question the propriety of a motion under consideration, a motion To Withdraw is in order. This procedure gives all members, including the presiding officer, more leeway to question the wisdom of considering a motion.

To Make a General or a Special Order

Robert's Rules of Order Newly Revised [3] devotes seven pages to discussing how questions become General Orders and Special Orders, and the complicated procedure for determining the priority or rank of these orders in the meeting to which they are assigned. Robert assumes that an organization's order of business will include the heading Orders of the Day, which designates questions whose consideration has been postponed to a certain day or hour. If a question is made a Special Order, which

---

3. *Roberts Rules of Order Newly Revised*, 9th ed. (Glenview, Ill.: ScottForesman, 1990), pp. 360≈366.

requires a two-thirds vote, all other business is suspended at the time designated to consider it.

This is an unnecessary procedure for voluntary organizations or for those that meet only annually. The secretary and other officers of such organizations can be trusted to see that items postponed until a particular meeting are on the agenda of that meeting, and are considered, without resorting to General Orders and Special Orders.

To Call for the Orders of the Day

To Call for the Orders of the Day is to remind the presiding officer to redirect the assembly's attention to the agenda from which it has wandered. Though customarily used in this way, its technical purpose is to remind the presiding officer that the time has arrived to consider a matter previously postponed. Since it is recommended that General and Special Orders be eliminated, To Call for the Orders of the Day is of little value.

A reminder to the presiding officer to adhere to the agenda is best accomplished by a request that needs no further translation, such as, "Madam Chairwoman, I believe we omitted the report of the treasurer."[4] If stronger measures are necessary to get the floor, a member may rise to a Point of Order to remind the presiding officer of the need to return to the agenda.

To Close Nominations

This motion is unnecessary. When it is in order, it is superfluous, since nominations have for all practical purposes already been closed; otherwise, it is premature and hence out of order. Both Robert and Sturgis state that a motion To Close Nominations is not required.[5] It

---

4. As recommended by Robert W. English in "Motions which Should be Abolished," *Parliamentary Journal* 5 (July 1964): 30≈31. English includes among motions that should be abolished all those included in this chapter except To Amend the Amendment, To Close Nominations, and To Make a General or Special Order.

5. *Robert's Rules*, p. 282; Sturgis, *The Standard Code*, p. 141.

should never be used to deprive a member of the right to nominate the candidate of her or his choice. Rather, Robert states that the chair should simply inquire whether there are any further nominations. If none are offered, the chair should declare the nominations closed.

The motion To Close Nominations serves as a routine signal that the election may now proceed. The alert presiding officer will not need to rely on the motion To Close Nominations, but at the appropriate time will say, "If there are no further nominations [pausing], we will proceed with voting on the nominees for the office of vice president. Will the tellers please distribute the ballots?"

To Reconsider and Have It Entered on the Minutes

This is another motion with an esoteric and questionable purpose; to permit a minority that regards itself as disadvantaged because absentee members prevent it from being a majority to render meaningless a decision by the majority. To be eligible to move To Reconsider the Vote on [stating the motion] and Have It Entered on the Minutes, according to Robert,[6] a member must have voted on the prevailing side of the motion whose vote is to be reconsidered; thus, recognizing certain defeat, a member may change his or her vote from the minority to the majority to establish eligibility to move To Reconsider and Have It Entered on the Minutes.

The effect of the motion To Reconsider and Have It Entered on the Minutes, if passed, is to prevent any action being taken on the decision in question until the vote on it is reconsidered at the next meeting. It is difficult to understand how a motion whose purpose is to prevent the rule of the majority from prevailing can be defended. Its use permits the minority to determine what constitutes valid action on the part of the majority. This contradicts a basic principle of parliamentary law, that of majority rule.

6. *Robert's Rules*, p. 328. Sturgis, among other authorities, no longer recognizes this procedure as having any validity; Sturgis, *The Standard Code*, p. 226.

To Expunge From the Record

This motion, if passed, requires the secretary to write across the section of the minutes in question the words "Expunged by action of [date]." The record itself is not erased. Since the action in question may be nullified by the motion To Rescind, the strong feeling implied in expunging from the record has little justification.

To Call for a Division of the Assembly

The purpose of this request is to check on the accuracy of an announced vote. A method of accomplishing this purpose must, of course, be retained, but the expression is archaic. Assemblies do not divide even when they are requested to. Instead, the presiding officer simply calls for another vote, using a method that provides for a more accurate count, such as a show of hands, a rising vote, or ballots. Thus, the purpose of this motion can be effected by a request that the vote be taken again, by another method, stated in clear language that requires no further explanation.

To Dispense With the Reading of the Minutes

The problem with this motion is to determine what it means. "To dispense with" usually means to do without, but the motion as commonly invoked makes no provision for the *approval* of the minutes. In its present form it is ambiguous and should be abandoned. Other more specifically worded motions may be substituted to fulfill related purposes, such as To Omit reading of the minutes and approve them as printed in the call for this meeting; To Refer the minutes for approval to the Executive Committee; To Postpone reading of the minutes and have them printed and distributed to the members for consideration at the next meeting; or To Refer the consideration of the minutes to the Organization and Rules Committee, which shall be authorized to approve the minutes or to make any changes necessary for accuracy.

Chapter 7

Conducting the Meeting

Role of the Presiding Officer

Impartiality

Most authorities agree that the presiding officer should remain impartial--particularly while administering parliamentary rules. But may he or she participate in the debate on a motion under consideration, and still be an impartial presiding officer? Many presiding officers openly offer "some remarks on the motion" while still in the chair, thoroughly shattering the image of impartiality, at least on the question under consideration.

While practically every presiding officer will, on occasion, reveal some partiality, either indirectly by attitude or directly by comments, to do so reduces his or her effectiveness as a presiding officer. If he or she wishes to speak for or against the adoption of a motion, the presiding officer owes it to the membership to step down at least to the same physical and psychological level as other members when participating in debate. This is done simply by requesting a vice president or another officer of the organization to "take the chair" during the discussion and vote on the motion under consideration. The chair is resumed routinely after the vote has been announced on the motion under consideration. This is a time-honored procedure, and a presiding officer of integrity who perceives the role accurately will recognize the obligation to relinquish the chair when he or she wishes to add to the discussion on a motion.

Duty to Preside

The procedural difficulties encountered by groups in decision making tend to vary inversely with the presiding officer's knowledge and skill in parliamentary procedure. This holds true, of course, only if the presiding officer evaluates her or his role as serving the group, striving for fair play among members, trying honestly to ascertain the intent of individuals and of the group as a whole, and providing guidance for the fulfillment of this intent. The effective presiding officer never forgets that she or he is the servant of the assembly, presiding at their pleasure, and the guardian of the assembly's rules of procedure.

The presiding officer must know the basic principles and essential rules of parliamentary procedure. This knowledge may be rudimentary, lacking the ready facility acquired only through practice, but the presiding officer cannot be excused from knowing the fundamentals required to present, modify, refer, and postpone motions, and to bring them to a vote in an orderly and efficient fashion.

Knowledge of how to conduct a meeting is, unfortunately, rarely a qualification for election to office. If this lack of knowledge continues, a wise and competent leader risks exposure to embarrassment, and even ridicule. In cases of extreme inability to conduct a meeting, the presiding officer may rely heavily on the parliamentarian, even to the extent of having the parliamentarian preside temporarily.

It is important that the presiding officer refuse to get "rattled" or confused about what is going on in the meeting. Any presiding officer who permits members to speak at will, to offer main motions when a main motion is already under consideration, to interrupt speakers, or to claim the floor without the recognition of the chair is failing in the role as leader. The effective presiding officer refuses to be interrupted after a motion has been proposed until he or she has either ruled the motion out of order or stated the motion and placed it before the assembly for discussion. To do otherwise is to invite turmoil.

An effective presiding officer, equally sensitive to the role of judge of acceptable procedure and to the emotional ramifications of judgment, never rules a member out of order as if delighted in her or his own authority and knowledge of the rules. No member deserves such harsh treatment.

Whenever the presiding officer rules a motion out of order, he or she should explain why it is out of order, and advise the mover when it would be in order, or how the mover's intent, if known, might be accomplished by the use of another procedure. The presiding officer might also assure the member that the assembly will return to the matter later, when the motion is in order.

Unlimited patience and a concern for fair play, attributes said to have been possessed in good measure by Henry M. Robert himself, are invaluable when presiding over meetings. Mrs. Henry M. Robert, Sr. relates the story of a man who traveled from Chicago to Milwaukee just to observe Robert presiding over a meeting. He evidently had been hoping for a grandiose performance, and returned to Chicago in disgust, saying, "Nothing happened...everything went like clockwork!"[1] No finer compliment could be paid to any presiding officer.

One cannot overemphasize that the presiding officer's attitude of objectivity and humanity must be genuine, and perceived as such by the assembly, if he or she is to be successful. In a very real sense, the way the presiding officer interprets the role will determine the "climate" of the group's deliberations.

---

1. See Joseph F. O'Brien, "Henry M. Robert as Presiding Officer," *Quarterly Journal of Speech* 42 (April 1956): 157≈162.

The Order of Business

Organizations should adopt, and include in their *rules of order*, a systematic plan for considering items in meetings. Such a plan is traditionally referred to as the *order of business*, agenda, calendar, or program. An organization is, of course, free to adopt any plan appropriate to its purpose and needs, but in the absence of special needs, the following plan may prove convenient:

Order of Business for a Session of an Assembly

1. Presentation of minutes
2. Reports of officers, boards, and standing committees
3. Reports of special committees
4. Unfinished business
5. New business

Such an order of business provides the needed structure for a meeting and serves to notify members when certain items may be expected to come up for consideration. Changing the order of business, when desired, is possible by general consent or by a two-thirds vote "To Suspend the Rules." (This procedure is outlined in the section on suspending the rules in Chapter 5.)

Recognition of Speakers

The presiding officer must be fair in recognizing speakers in debate. There is nothing wrong with the time-honored custom of awarding the floor first to the mover of the motion in question or to the member to whom she or he relinquishes this privilege. This is a bit of parliamentary courtesy that is appreciated and deserved.

As a rule, the presiding officer should allow for alternation of speakers pro and con on motions under consideration. He or she should recognize, however, that some members who deserve a hearing are neither pro nor con. Those who have needed technical information should testify as experts. Others may wish to present a compromise or an amendment to salvage the desirable aspects of a motion and discard the undesirable ones. Therefore, the presiding officer cannot always proceed as if there were only two sides to an issue.

The presiding officer should guard against recognizing "big shots" to the exclusion of not-so-well-known members who wish to share in the discussion. And he or she should be ready to refuse firmly to recognize members who claim the floor a second or third time before others have had their first turn to speak. Members will respect a presiding officer who is scrupulously fair in administering parliamentary rules even if, on occasion, some of them feel piqued; but they will be quick to blame the presiding officer who shows partisanship in awarding the floor.

Disciplinary Measures

It sometimes becomes necessary for the presiding officer to assume leadership in keeping order in the assembly. If a nonmember is at the center of a disturbance, the presiding officer may invite the offender, after appropriate warning, to leave the meeting; this action is a ruling from the chair and may be appealed by a member, but not by the nonmember. Disturbances may be in the nature of continued interruption of speakers, heckling, slander, profane language, and the like. An organization has the authority to control its own meeting and to determine who, if anyone, may be present other than its own members.

It is imperative that the presiding officer remain calm in such circumstances and in no case indulge in shouting or frantic gavel-hammering to quiet a disturber. If the occasion requires it, the presiding officer may state his or her willingness to entertain a motion to exclude all nonmembers from the meeting...sometimes called a motion To Go into Executive Session. This is a nondebatable motion that may not be amended and requires a majority vote to pass.

Disturbances by members may also require the presiding officer to take action. Particularly obstreperous members may be requested by the presiding officer to make less noise. Members who demand the floor after exhausting their rights to debate or, worse, continue to talk without having been recognized by the chair must be dealt with. A warning from the presiding officer should suffice. A second unheeded warning should alert the presiding officer that more drastic action is needed, and she or he may direct the member to be seated. If necessary, the presiding officer may invite a motion to censure the offending member, explaining that this becomes a matter of record in the minutes of the organization. If offered, the motion is debatable and should require a two-thirds vote to pass. Likewise, a motion to exclude a member from the meeting is debatable and requires a two-thirds vote. The offending member should be permitted to speak in his or her own defense, and the secretary may be called on to read examples of offensive remarks that were recorded during the proceedings.

Members excluded from a meeting by vote of the assembly, but who refuse to leave, invite more serious action by the assembly. The presiding officer may appoint other members to escort the offending member from the meeting, or the local police may be called to remove him or her. The organization should be prepared to press formal charges if such extreme action is necessary. If it is anticipated that serious trouble may occur in a meeting, it is probably wise to alert the police and to request the presence of police officers.

The presiding officer alone has no authority to discipline members but may conduct the procedures for disciplining members at the direction of the assembly. In fact, the presiding officer may actually be disciplined or removed from office, a procedure explained in Chapter 20 of *Robert's Rules*, which also outlines methods for formally charging members with offenses, preparing defenses, and conducting trials.

Voting Procedures

As a member of the group, the presiding officer has the same right to vote as any other member. However, it is probably wise for the presiding officer to vote only in cases in which a vote is needed to change the outcome. Thus, he or she may vote to break or create a tie, and to prevent or make possible a two-thirds vote. The presiding officer should always participate when the vote is by secret ballot, whether or not he or she wishes to write anything on the ballot.

The conventional procedures for handling motions should be carefully followed by the presiding officer, largely to ensure that all members understand what is under consideration and what is being voted on. Assuming an uncomplicated motion such as "that we give ten dollars to the Red Cross" has been made by a member, the presiding officer should follow these steps:

1. The presiding officer states the motion and invites discussion.

    Chair: The motion that we give ten dollars to the Red Cross is now before you. Is there any discussion?

2. Discussion ended, the presiding officer restates the motion in its final form and asks for the affirmative vote followed by the negative vote. That order is never reversed.

    Chair: If there is no further discussion, we are now voting on the motion that we give ten dollars to the Red Cross. Those in favor of the motion, please say "aye." Those opposed, say "no." (If preferred, the words "yes" and "no" may be used.)

3. The presiding officer announces the result of the voting and adds any necessary information to interpret or to effect the decision.

    Chair: The motion is carried, and the treasurer will present our check for ten dollars to the local Red Cross.
    or
    The motion is lost [or defeated] and we have decided against the motion that

would have us give ten dollars to the Red
Cross. The next item on our agenda is. . . .

All of these steps are essential for clarity. Since
considerable time may elapse between Steps 1 and 2, and
changes may be made to the motion as presented in Step
1, it is imperative that Step 2 be followed to the letter.
Omission or abridgement of Step 2 has caused many a
member to murmur, "Hey, just what are we voting on?"
or to abstain from voting out of confusion.

Chairperson by Decree

If the presiding officer is not elected by the assembly but
appointed, as in the case of some chairpersons of boards
of corporations, university presidents, and college deans,
he or she is known as a *chairperson by decree*.[2] To expect
impartiality of such individuals is unrealistic; they are
serving two masters, and their first loyalty is probably to
the authority to whom they owe their position. What
may be expected in such cases is precise definition of the
assembly's legitimate areas of jurisdiction, and an
agreed-upon division of responsibilities, so that the presiding officer is not put in the precarious position of
presiding over the consideration of motions that threat-
en his or her relationship with superiors or his or her
very position. We delude ourselves if we expect impartiality under these circumstances.

When the presiding officer of a group is a power
figure, perhaps one to whom the rank-and-file members
owe their positions, current status, and salary incre-
ments, they are forced to settle for something less than
normal freedom in decision making. Such a group is not
democratic because of the inequality of membership. The

---

2. See Ray E. Keesey, "Chairman by Decree," *Parliamentary Journal* 10
   (July 1969): 3≈6, for a further discussion of the anomalous situation
   of a chairperson who was not elected by the assembly he or she
   presides over. William S. Tacey, in "Chairman by Decree Ousted,"
   Parliamentary Journal 10 (October 1969): 20≈23, suggests meeting
   this situation in college faculties by allowing the faculty to elect its
   own presiding officer.

bylaws of such an organization should protect both the presiding officer and the membership by spelling out in detail the authority granted the presiding officer that does not stem from the membership. And the members have a right to know, and to have stated in the bylaws, the limitations under which they must operate. It is well to remember that a meeting conducted by a chairperson by decree is equally difficult for both parties, the presiding officer and the members.

Participating Members

The members of an organization who participate actively in its deliberations will find their contributions considerably enhanced if they are familiar with basic procedure. With a simplified procedure, it is not too much to expect that members be familiar with the ordinary motions used to amend, refer, and postpone; to limit and close debate; and to recess and adjourn. These procedures are more than will be required in most meetings.

In addition to knowing parliamentary procedure, members are expected to exhibit just and orderly behavior. Members will abide by decisions of the chair (unless an appeal is in order), refrain from discrediting individuals when they should be attacking arguments, exercise courtesy toward others, be restrained in language and action, and cheerfully (on the surface, at least) work to implement a majority decision even if they voted with the minority.

The Secretary

The *secretary* keeps the official record. He or she should be seated close to the presiding officer and observe carefully all that occurs as he or she takes notes, later to be rewritten in the form desired by the organization. The secretary is the presiding officer's "right hand," providing her or him with a copy of the agenda; the minutes of the previous meeting; committee reports, if available; and a list of unfinished business. The secretary brings to the meeting materials that may be needed, such as the minute book of the organization, up-to-date copies of the bylaws, and a quantity of ballots.

The secretary should know the previous legislative record of the organization and should serve as a source of information for the presiding officer and members when questions arise about actions previously taken. The secretary brings an official roster of the membership to the meeting. In addition, the secretary should be familiar with parliamentary procedure and be able, on occasion, to preside in the absence of the usual presiding officer.

The *minutes* of an organization include a record of all official actions taken, the presiding officer, the presence of a quorum, and information showing that the meeting was duly called and thus legal. The other contents of the minutes will depend upon the degree of detail desired. Some organizations go to the extreme of recording the name of each member who presents a motion, major ideas presented in the discussion, and the numerical count on all votes. Such details are rarely needed and only make the job of the secretary difficult. The exact statement of motions passed should be recorded; the names of participants in the discussion of the motion need not be. It is desirable to include in the minutes the major arguments for and against a motion, but these should not be identified with speakers proposing them since the privilege of discussing a motion freely is jeopardized when what is said becomes a part of public record. Furthermore, what the vote was or who offered the motion is probably not significant ten years later. The minutes should be an *official record of actions taken* by the organization, not a transcript of what individuals say in meetings.

Likewise, motions proposed, discussed, and voted down may or may not be entered in the minutes. Complete records must be kept, of course, of all referrals, postponements, and appeals. Amendments need not be entered. If one imagines examining the record ten or twenty years later, a clearer perspective emerges on what is essential. The most common error is to record too much.

If the secretary is a member of the organization, he or she has the same right to present, discuss, and vote on motions as any other member.

The Parliamentarian

The *parliamentarian*, who advises the presiding officer on parliamentary procedure, should be a specialist, by knowledge and experience. She or he should be appointed by the presiding officer, not elected. It is probably better if they are not a member of the organization, since they must be objective and impartial advisers. If they are members of the organization, they are entitled to their rights...although they cannot exercise them and still remain impartial. They should vote in all secret ballot votes, but in other instances they vote only at risk of losing their image of impartiality. Many organizations, particularly those that hold state, regional, and national conventions, engage a paid professional parliamentarian.[3]

The parliamentarian's work begins prior to the meeting in which she or he advises the presiding officer. As a condition of accepting an appointment, the parliamentarian should be provided with an up-to-date copy of the bylaws, the program for the meeting in which she or he is to serve, a copy of the minutes of the previous meeting, and any other information that may help orient her or him to the organization. The presiding officer and the parliamentarian should meet informally before the meeting to discuss parliamentary problems that may arise, to determine the extent to which the presiding officer is likely to need help, and to brief the parliamentarian on possible sources of parliamentary intrigue, cliques, emotional issues, self-appointed parliamentary strategists, and the like. The parliamentarian may also be available to advise members who request assistance on motions

---

3. The American Institute of Parliamentarians maintains a directory of certified professional parliamentarians drawn from its membership. Write to Executive Director, 203 West Wayne Street, Suite 312, Ft. Wayne, IN 46802.

they wish to present, acceptable procedures, and legitimate strategy to attain desired ends.

The parliamentarian should be easily accessible to the presiding officer during the meeting, preferably seated next to him or her on the platform. The parliamentarian gives advice on procedure when requested by the presiding officer. It is not unusual for a member to "request a ruling by the parliamentarian" on whether or not a motion is in order, or on some other procedural question. The parliamentarian replies in private to the presiding officer who may, if he wishes, pass on what the parliamentarian has said. The parliamentarian does not answer questions by addressing the assembly, except at the invitation of the presiding officer. She or he does not make "rulings" even though requested to do so but may provide information to assist the presiding officer in making a ruling.

The effective parliamentarian is constantly alert, following closely the progress of the group in handling its agenda. She or he knows what the immediately pending motion is at all times and keeps track of motions by using one of the various methods of notetaking for parliamentary proceedings. The parliamentarian must be quick to call the attention of the presiding officer, as unobtrusively as possible, to errors in procedure, and to advise him or her on correcting the procedure. The parliamentarian must not sit by while serious procedural errors persist, lest there develop a hopeless mess from which the only escape is to disregard pending motions and start over again.

On the other hand, the parliamentarian should not be so fastidious in insisting on letter-perfect procedure that she or he becomes a nuisance. The experienced parliamentarian takes a stand in between the two extremes and often earns the sincere plaudits of an audience appreciative of her or his help.

Other Officials

The vice president or vice presidents, the president-elect,

the executive secretary, the corresponding secretary, the treasurer, and perhaps the sergeant at arms all occupy positions of significance. Most of these officers, however, do not usually exercise their functions directly in organizational meetings; an exception is the sergeant at arms, and many groups do not have one. Organizations having these officers should spell out in the bylaws their functions, the conditions of their appointment or election, terms of office, procedures for filling vacancies, and the like; it is not necessary to enlarge upon them here.[4]

---

4. This additional information is available in, among other sources, Alice Sturgis, *The Standard Code of Parliamentary Procedure*, 3rd ed. (New York: McGraw-Hill, 1988), pp. 156≈165.

Chapter 8

Committees

Much of the actual work of many organizations is done by committees. It has been said that organizations meet largely to approve what their committees have done. The wisdom of consideration by committee is clear when one recalls that a committee functions with certain inherent advantages over a large assembly. The committee is smaller; operates more informally; is composed of members selected for their competence, knowledge, and willingness to do a particular job; and can go about its work of investigating, holding hearings, and interviewing experts quietly and efficiently. It does the work of the assembly more effectively, and then reports its recommendations.

In spite of all the jokes about committees and some organizations' propensity to form committees at the slightest pretext, the practice of referring considerations to committees is sound. This chapter will look more closely at various kinds of committees and at some aspects of their functioning.

Standing and Special Committees

Standing committees are provided for in the bylaws of an organization. They remain in existence even though their membership may change with the expiration of terms of office. Most organizations have standing committees for such matters as membership, program, bylaw revision, finance, public relations, and the like.

Special committees are those appointed or elected to do a particular job; they cease to exist when they have reported to the assembly. The members may be appointed by the presiding officer or elected by the assembly. The size of the committee, the selection process, and the deadline for reporting may all be stipulated in the motion referring consideration to a committee. The person who presides over a special committee may be named by the organization's presiding officer when he appoints the members, may be elected by the committee's members, or may be elected by the assembly. It is common practice for the members of a special committee to be announced by the presiding officer in the meeting in which the committee is authorized...with the first-named member assuming its chair.

Selection of Members

The first consideration in assuring a committee's success is wise selection of its members, a factor that may take on increased importance when evaluating the report submitted by the committee. The members should be those most competent and willing to do the task assigned to the committee. If a committee is organized to fulfill a purpose or develop a project already approved by the assembly, its members should obviously be chosen from among those in favor of the proposal.

Other considerations should be kept in mind when selecting committee members. Ordinarily, the committee should be representative of the assembly...that is, its members should represent various interest groups, geographical areas, occupations, and the like. In addition, care should be exercised not to assign a given member to many committees just because he or she is a willing worker. A committee should normally not be composed entirely of new members of the organization. And its members should be free to devote adequate time to the work of the committee, within the agreed-upon time limits. To prevent a tie vote, most committees should be composed of an odd number of members. The committee should be no larger than necessary, within the limitations imposed by the other considerations mentioned above.

Sometimes the bylaws specify that the organization's president, or another official, shall be an *ex officio* member of all committees or boards; such membership is granted by virtue of office. *Ex officio* membership usually confers all the privileges of other committee members, including the right to vote, but not the obligation to attend meetings regularly. Therefore, unless present, an *ex officio* member should not be counted in determining a quorum.

The presiding officer of a committee needs an understanding of the process of decision making in small groups, as well as special competence in the subject of the committee's work. He or she needs patience, a willingness to delegate work to others, and an appreciation of the necessity for record-keeping and for writing a report that fairly represents the views of the committee. The presiding officer of a committee may serve as the committee's secretary, as do presiding officers of small committees, or he or she may appoint a member to serve as secretary. Skill in human relations...the ability to draw out reticent members and prevent more assertive members from dominating the meetings...will stand the presiding officer in good stead. He or she needs to recognize the necessity of reminding members of their task when digression threatens to be too time consuming, and, likewise, the beneficial effects of an occasional brief digression in minimizing individual differences that have reached the argumentative stage. While not appearing to hurry deliberations, the presiding officer gently presses the committee toward its assigned goal.

Procedure in Committees

There is little need for formal parliamentary procedure in committee meetings. The informality typical of a small discussion group is ideal, provided, of course, that it is not carried to the point of interfering with the committee's progress. The presiding officer sets the tone of the meeting. He or she should prepare an agenda that includes a statement of the committee's purpose and should ask for the members' approval of the agenda at the beginning of the meeting. This may not be required in meetings of standing committees, but should not be omitted in special committees.

On occasion, votes must be taken and actions recorded. Usually votes can be taken fairly by general consent at the point when the presiding officer recognizes that the members are in agreement and ready to have that agreement recorded. Unless otherwise stipulated in the bylaws, the quorum for a committee is a majority of its membership.

Informality should prevail in the statement, and possible modifications, of motions. Sometimes a formal statement of a motion is necessary only to reach consensus on how the committee's agreement should be stated in its report. It is a good idea to discuss the wording of a motion informally, instead of following the formal procedure of stating a motion and amending it by vote.

There is usually no time limit on discussion in committee meetings, but the presiding officer should tactfully ensure that certain members do not do all the talking. The presiding officer may participate freely in discussion, without the restriction on her or his participation in debate usually found in meetings of the assembly.

The committee's presiding officer should ascertain exactly what has been accomplished in each meeting. Before adjourning, the presiding officer should seek the committee's approval of the notation she or he plans to make in the record of its achievements at the meeting. The notation should include special assignments to committee members to carry on investigations independently, consultants to be interviewed, and special sources to be checked, as well as agreements reached at the meeting and plans for the next meeting. A majority of the committee members present must approve the final report before it may be submitted to the assembly.

Committee Reports

The form of a committee's report will vary with its function. A committee appointed to do something, purchase something, conduct an investigation, or take action for the assembly will write a report setting forth what was done or purchased, the results of its investigation, or the action taken. For example, a committee appointed to investigate available public address systems and authorized to purchase and have installed in the clubhouse their choice of a new public address system might report as follows:

> Your committee appointed to investigate available public address systems and to purchase the choice recommended by the committee has held two meetings with all members present. The committee has also visited three local audio-electrical appliance companies and had these three submit written bids, drawn to committee specifications, for the public address system. The three bids were reviewed and compared with committee specifications by a special consultant engaged by the committee, whom the committee paid a fee of $150. Her recommendation was to purchase the PA system from Dunn Brothers Audio Incorporated, whose bid was $1,600 after installation. Your committee has agreed to this purchase, and the equipment, with a year's guarantee, will be installed on Friday of this week.

Because the committee report summarizes action previously authorized by the assembly, no further action need be taken on the report, except to file it for future reference.

More frequently, however, a committee report includes both a summary of its proceedings and recommendations for proposed action to be taken by the assembly. This occurs when a motion is passed to refer the consideration of a pending main motion to a standing committee or special committee for study and recommendations to guide the assembly.

For example, a city council meeting referred a main motion "that the wattage be doubled in all city lights on Main Street" to a special committee to study and present recommendations. The committee report might take the following form:

> Your committee, to which was referred the main motion "that the wattage be doubled in all city lights on Main Street," wishes to report that the committee has met with representatives of the Diamond Electric Company, which provides the city with electric power; with the city police committee on crime prevention and control, and with the executive committee of the City Board of Education, and recommends that the motion mentioned be rejected as an oversimplification of the problem. If rejected, the committee will propose a motion to upgrade the city lighting system on a selective basis, increasing the power or lights in areas where crime has increased generally, and will recommend several new installations of lights on city streets. However, the motion to be proposed by the committee is too complicated to arrive at by amending the pending motion and the committee, therefore, recommends that the pending motion be defeated.

In its present form, this report need only be filed, perhaps with the thanks of the council for a job well done. The council, with the advice of its committee fresh in mind, would continue consideration of the main motion, perhaps heeding the committee's recommendation to reject it. If so, the council's presiding officer would normally then turn to the presiding officer of the committee and offer him or her an opportunity to present the new motion the committee promised would be forthcoming if the previous main motion were defeated. Thus the promised recommendation of the committee becomes a main motion, treated like any other main motion and subject to any of the motions (amending, referring, postponing, limiting or closing debate, withdrawing) the council may wish to apply to its consideration.

The report of a committee appointed to set the time, place, and date for an annual meeting, and to suggest broad outlines for the meeting's program, should be adopted, not filed, if approved by the assembly; in this case, the assembly's adoption is necessary to commit the organization to fulfillment of such actions.

Committee reports may be oral or written, depending upon the degree of formality desired, the difficulty of the subject matter, and the need for written records. A special committee appointed to look into the desirability of holding a group picnic at a certain place and time may present a brief oral report summarizing its findings to the parent group. On the other hand, a committee report on the wisdom of establishing regional conventions, a national headquarters, or a change in basic organizational policy would normally be written and detailed. A written report, especially on important considerations, takes the form of an impersonal communication in the third person addressed to the president and signed by the presiding officer for the committee. It may begin,

> Your committee to investigate and recommend with regard to [stating the committee's charge] wishes to report as follows:

A minority report, if submitted, may take a similar form, such as,

> The undersigned, not agreeing with the majority of the committee, present a minority report as follows:

To the extent that the committee report is a factual account of the committee's deliberations, expert counsel, hearings, site visitations, subcommittee investigations, and the like, there is no need for a minority report. It is when the committee report enters into the realm of opinion, offering advice to the assembly, that a minority report may be legitimate. Therefore, a minority report will usually include a statement of intent to offer recommendations in the form of main motions that differ from those presented in the committee report. The assembly's approval of the minority report as a substitute for the committee report is understood not to apply to the factual portion of the committee report, only to the recommendations to be presented as main motions for action by the assembly.

In general, formal minority reports are seldom necessary, since any committee member may present to the assembly an opinion that differs from that of the committee. That is, members may propose an amendment to any of the committee's recommendations presented as a main motion for assembly action. They may also announce their intentions to do so during discussion of the committee report. Note that the term *committee report*, not *majority committee report*, is used to refer to the report submitted by a majority of the committee, even if a minority report is filed.

Presentation and Consideration of Reports

Reports from standing committees usually precede those of special committees in the order of business. Standing committees' reports are often presented in the order in which they are listed in the bylaws. The reports of special committees are presented either in the order in which the committees were appointed or in an order determined for each meeting.

The organization's presiding officer usually calls for a committee report by announcing that the report of the (naming the committee) will be presented at this time. Whether or not he or she names the presiding officer of the committee, it is assumed, unless an announcement is made to the contrary, that the presiding officer of the committee will present the report. The committee's presiding officer should already have provided the secretary with a copy of the committee report.

If the report is long, it should have been duplicated and distributed with the call for the meeting; in this case, the presiding officer of the committee may assume that the report has been read, and may ask for discussion without reading it. If the report is routine...consisting of a record of meetings held, topics discussed, and the expected fulfillment of functions assigned, and recommending no action...the committee's presiding officer may simply say, "Our committee's report is printed in the call for the meeting. I will be glad to answer any questions on the report." Following the discussion, if there is any, the presiding officer of the organization should announce, "Since no action is required, the report will be filed."

In order to avoid confusion, it must be clearly stated in the committee's report that its recommendations will be presented in the form of main motions following consideration of the report. The adoption of a committee report which includes recommendations later to be presented as main motions does not commit the assembly to implementing those recommendations. When the committee's recommendations are presented as a main motion, it should not be stated as, "I move adoption of the committee's recommendations that . . .," but, like any other main motion, as "I move that. . . ." This is essential, since the adoption of a committee's recommendation is entirely different than the authorization of an action proposed in the form of a main motion.

Usually, the consideration of a committee report is fairly routine. The report of a committee's deliberations may not be amended, except to correct errors of fact since the assembly may not make the committee say something that it did not say. Of course, clarification may be requested, and the report may be discussed, filed, adopted, rejected, or sent back to the committee for further study, and its consideration may be postponed to a more convenient time.

In the interest of clarity, committee reports should normally be filed, or, if applicable, adopted, but not *received* or *accepted,* since the latter terms are ambiguous and mean different things to different people.

An informational report or progress report should usually not be adopted. To *file* a committee report makes it available to the members for reference, and for reconsideration if necessary, but commits the assembly to nothing. To *adopt* a report commits the assembly to approval of opinions and activities described but does not authorize implementation of its proposed recommendations.

As stated earlier, committees' recommendations are

presented as main motions. If a motion is long and controversial, such as a motion to adopt changes in the bylaws presented by a bylaw-revision committee, it may be considered "by paragraph." The term *paragraph* should be taken to refer not to the literary paragraph but to any subdivision of content that may not be further divided; more than one literary paragraph may constitute a subdivision.

The committee's presiding officer reads or...if they have copies of the report...directs the members' attention to "paragraph one," and then pauses while the presiding officer of the organization inquires if there is discussion. The committee may be requested to supply additional information, and an amendment may be proposed, handled like any other proposed amendment, and voted on. Several changes may be authorized this way. When there is no further discussion, the presiding officer directs the committee's presiding officer to proceed with "paragraph two," and so on. A vote is not taken on *the adoption* of paragraph one at this time, although votes on proposed amendments to it may have been taken.

When all the paragraphs have been presented, discussed, and modified to please the assembly, the committee's presiding officer asks for discussion, or further amendments, of *any paragraph in the report*, before the motion "that the changes in the bylaws be adopted" is voted on. The required vote to pass a motion to amend the bylaws would be that stipulated in the bylaws.

Minority reports, which may also be distributed with the call for the meeting, are presented by the spokesperson for the minority, who moves that the minority's recommendations be substituted for those in the committee report wherever applicable. This is a proposed amendment to the committee report and is handled like any other proposed amendment. It should be offered immediately after presentation of the committee report, or immediately after the presiding officer of the committee announces that the committee report is printed in the call for the meeting and is therefore open to discussion. The minority's recommendations, in the form of a substitute amendment, become the immediately pending motion; if passed by a majority vote, they are incorporated into the committee report, replacing the majority's recommendations, which are simply filed for reference.

If the spokespersons for the committee report and for the minority report plan to present recommendations as main motions following their reports, it is helpful to have them announce their intention to do so before presenting their reports. They may also indicate informally what these motions will involve, if this information has not already been distributed in printed form.

When an assembly refers the consideration of a motion to a committee…standing or special…the report of the committee should include an accurate statement of the motion referred and the results of the committee's work. A proposed amendment pending when referral was made to the committee is still pending when the committee reports back to the assembly, and the committee may recommend its passage or rejection. The committee may suggest that other changes be made, and may announce its intention to offer amendments after the pending amendment is disposed of. The committee may also propose its own improved version of the referred motion as a substitute amendment. It is important to recognize that the committee report is offered as advice to the assembly and that even if it is filed or adopted, the assembly still must take official action by voting on the main motion that was originally referred to the committee.

Information on Committees in the Bylaws

All standing committees should be named in the constitution or bylaws. (See Chapter 11 for the distinction between the constitution and the bylaws.) For each committee, the following information should be provided:

1. Number of members, and number constituting a quorum.

2. Special qualifications, if any, for membership.

3. Selection process for members.
4. Selection process for the presiding officer.
5. Terms of office, including provision for "staggering" terms if desired.
6. Function.
7. Provision for filling vacancies.
8. Frequency and time of reports.

The bylaws should also authorize the president or the assembly to create special committees to accomplish particular tasks. The structure of special committees cannot be set forth in the bylaws since it will depend upon the purpose and nature of the committee.

In summary, the presentation and consideration of committees' reports often leads to confusion, much of which could be prevented if organizations spelled out in their bylaws that a committee's recommendations requiring action by the assembly must be presented as separate main motions for consideration and vote by the assembly.

Chapter 9

Voting

Types of Votes

The Majority Vote

When an impatient member of an assembly says, "Let's put it to a vote," referring to the motion under consideration, he or she is asking the presiding officer to determine the majority vote. A *majority vote* is a majority of eligible votes cast, not counting blanks and abstentions; unless there are special stipulations to the contrary, this is the definition of majority vote that should be applied.

The term has several possible meanings, however, and the bylaws of an organization should stipulate the particular meaning intended if a special definition is applicable. There are at least six different definitions of majority votes:

1. A majority of the eligible votes cast
2. A majority of the members present and voting (same as Number 1)
3. A majority of the members present
4. A majority of the members in good standing

5. A majority of a quorum

6. A majority of the membership. This is usually applied to a group with a small fixed membership, such as a State Board of Health, and a prescribed majority, such as a requirement that five of the eight members vote in favor of a motion to carry it, whether or not all members are in attendance.

Decisions may be made by only a small number of the members in attendance. Since members may choose not to vote...that is, to abide by the majority decision...it is possible for a majority vote to represent only a small fraction of the number in attendance. With one hundred members in attendance, the following all represent legal majority votes: 80 to 20, 40 to 10, 20 to 5, 10 to 9, 5 to 3, and 1 to 0.

The Unanimous Vote

Strictly speaking, a *unanimous vote* should mean that all members present and eligible to vote did so, and that all voted the same way. Some liberty is taken with the definition when a presiding officer announces a "unanimous decision" following a vote by general consent. To say that a member did not object is different than saying that he or she voted.

A more accurate announcement of the results of such a vote would be, "The motion is carried without objection," or "The motion is carried without any dissenting votes." When a member chooses not to vote, and to abide by the decision formed by those who do vote, it is not accurate to announce a decision that suggests she or he did vote.

It is recommended that the term "by unanimous vote" not be used carelessly. Members may be offended, but not wish to protest its misuse openly. Organizations have been known to pass a motion by majority vote and then, under the impression that it would look better on the record, agree to make the vote unanimous if no one objects. Very little sober reflection is needed to condemn this practice. It offends the basic principle of equality of membership, which guarantees each member the right to vote or to abstain from voting without having to reveal which he or she did.

The practice of declaring a member who is elected to office by secret ballot as "elected by unanimous vote," if no one objects, fools no one and should likewise be condemned. For the secretary to "cast a unanimous ballot" for a candidate, even if he or she is unopposed, should never be condoned. A unanimous vote should mean just what it says.

A Two-thirds Vote

A *two-thirds vote*, used in controlling debate and in votes so stipulated in the bylaws, usually means two thirds of the eligible votes cast. Other definitions include all the variations listed under the discussion of the majority vote, if one substitutes two thirds for a majority. In the arithmetic of determining a two-thirds vote, final fractions are given a full vote. For example, two thirds of fourteen is considered to be ten, as is two thirds of fifteen; one third of fourteen is considered to be five, the number necessary to defeat a motion requiring two thirds if only fourteen votes are cast. For a motion that requires two-thirds vote to pass, there must be twice as many votes in the affirmative as in the negative, or 60 to 30, 10 to 5, 4 to 2, or 2 to 1.

The Plurality Vote

A *plurality* is the highest number of votes received when more than two items or nominees are being voted on, whether or not this number represents a majority of the total votes cast. For example, if 10, 8, and 4 votes are cast for A, B, and C respectively, A has a plurality; no one has a majority (12 votes). If only one issue is under consideration, or if only two candidates are running in an election, the principle of majority rule applies. A plurality vote is not sufficient to pass a motion or to elect a member to office unless the bylaws of the organizations so provide.

The Tie Vote

In a *tie vote*, the total vote cast is equally divided between the affirmative and the negative, or between two or more candidates. A tie vote is considered a negative vote, not a "deadlock"; it does not pass a motion or elect a candidate to office. If the presiding officer has not already voted, he is eligible to vote. If the tie is not broken, the effect is the same as if the motion had lost by a majority vote in the negative or, in the case of an election, as if no vote had been taken.

An exception to the rule that a tie vote is treated as a negative vote occurs when the vote on an appeal from a ruling of the chair results in a tie. Since a majority vote is required to overrule the chair, a tie vote sustains the ruling of the chair.

Changing a Vote

Any member may change her or his vote before the results are announced, except when the vote is taken by ballot. When the ballots have been collected after voting, it is too late for a vote to be changed.

The Right Not to Vote: Abstaining

It is widely asserted that members have a duty to vote to express their willingness to share in the responsibility of decisions. But no one can be compelled to vote. If he or she wishes, a member may remain silent in a voice vote, answer "Present" in a roll call vote, or turn in a blank ballot. To abstain from voting, of course, is to help the winning side. Members who do so are bound by the decision of the majority. By not voting, they are, in effect, expressing their willingness to abide by the decision arrived at by the prevailing side.

Sometimes a member will insist that their abstention be officially recorded. They want the record to show that they did not vote on the motion under consideration. While some people think this is making too much of the privilege of not voting, organizations usually oblige such requests, "if there are no objections," by asking the secretary to record the names of members who abstain from voting. If this practice becomes a problem by delaying unnecessarily the taking of votes, the organization should formulate a policy on recording abstentions and incorporate it into the bylaws.

If a member's personal or financial interest in the outcome of a vote warrants a request that the record show her or his abstention from voting, the practice is, of course, defensible. On the other hand, any widespread practice of recording abstentions would appear to reflect a misunderstanding of the true meaning of exercising the privilege not to vote.

Methods of Voting

General Consent

Voting by general consent is not the same as voting by unanimous consent, and the presiding officer should not request unanimous votes or unanimous approval on even the most routine matters. In a vote by general consent, the presiding officer declares a motion passed or a request granted "if there is no objection." This is a common procedure and may, in the hands of a skillful presiding officer, be used to expedite the handling of business.

The procedure should be widely used to secure decisions on routine, noncontroversial questions. A presiding officer who is responsive to the generally known wishes of an assembly, and who can accurately detect the "sense of the meeting," may make frequent use of votes by general consent. The method constitutes a legal vote, and motions passed in this way should be recorded by the secretary as official actions.

Misuse of votes by general consent may be, and should be, prevented by any member or members saying, "I object." A single objection forces the presiding officer to take a vote that may be verified by count.

The Voice Vote

Presiding officers vary in the exact words they prefer to put a motion to a vote. Some, after stating the motion to be voted on, announce, "Those in favor of the motion, say Aye. Those opposed, No." Or, "Those in favor, make it manifest by saying Aye. Those voting against the motion, say No." The simplest statement consistent with maximum clarity is the best. A *voice vote* is an oral vote. It is the most frequently used method of voting in organizations of all sizes.

There are limitations, however, to voting by voice when a close vote is anticipated, because of the difficulty of counting the vote. The presiding officer who expects a fairly close vote on a motion saves time in the long run by requesting a vote by show of hands. This will also obviate the problem that arises when a loud minority outshouts a docile majority. The presiding officer should be quick to announce his or her own confusion in determining the results of such a voice vote, and should request another vote by show of hands. Of course, any member who has reason to question the presiding officer's count of a vote may request that he or she verify the accuracy of the announcement of a vote.

The Show of Hands

The advantage of voting by a show of hands is accuracy. In groups of up to two hundred people, and sometimes more, the presiding officer may count hands her- or himself, if there is a clear view of the whole assembly. For larger groups it is preferable to appoint tellers to count assigned sections of voters and to report the results to the chief teller or directly to the presiding officer. In large groups in which considerable time is required to count the votes, the presiding officer should probably direct members to "raise your right hand until counted," to alert them against dropping their hands too quickly. The count is accomplished more easily if all members vote by raising their right hands, since the hands are more evenly spaced.

In practice, most votes in large meetings can be quickly and quietly taken by a show of hands, and it is usually a waste of time to count since most votes are overwhelmingly pro or con. Voting by a show of hands helps to maintain decorum in large meetings, since voice votes may be quite noisy. Even a standing vote can usually be taken without counting.

The form varies. Many presiding officers, after stating the motion, announce, "Those in favor, please raise your right hands." After counting (if it appears necessary), the presiding officer signals for them to drop their hands by saying, "Thank you. [pause] Those opposed, please raise your right hands." And again, after counting, "Thank you." Then the presiding officer announces the result of the vote.

The Rising Vote

Though seldom necessary, a rising vote is sometimes used to express an emotion, such as gratitude, through "a rising vote of thanks" to someone. It is often used to express respect for a deceased member by voting "to spread on the minutes" a memorial statement outlining her or his accomplishments and the grief of the organization at her or his death.

In cases of extreme difficulty in determining a vote count by other means, members may be asked to vote by rising, or even to separate into two groups, one affirmative and one negative.

The Roll Call

Most people have witnessed dull and time-consuming roll call votes at televised national political conventions. It is a slow method of voting, although often considered the most accurate, and is justified only when it is desirable to make public the members' votes. It is sometimes used as a dilatory tactic by members who hope that the prospect of a roll call vote will cause members to leave, or that some members may balk at publicly recording their votes.

By Ballot

The ballot is used for voting in elections and for deciding issues that are emotionally charged and controversial. When it is desirable to conceal one's vote, the ballot may be used. Its use may be ordered on any motion by a majority vote on a nondebatable, nonamendable motion stating the method of voting to be used. Ideally, ballots are prepared in advance and a member has only to check his or her preference or preferences. The use of blank ballots is facilitated by writing on a blackboard the names and numbers of the candidates, or other choices, and asking the voter to write the number or numbers of his or her choice on the ballot.

Tellers collect the ballots and canvass (see page 118) them, counting blanks separately; they then report the results...votes for, against, illegal, and blank...to the presiding officer, who announces the results. Marked but invalid (illegal) votes are counted in the total votes cast to determine a majority; blank votes are ignored in the total count. Many organizations could make wiser use of the ballot method of voting by employing preferential voting, discussed on pages 120≈123.

The Mail Vote

A vote by mail may be ordered by a majority vote, provided the bylaws permit this procedure. The bylaws should also specify those responsible for preparing and distributing ballots, the procedure to be followed by the voter in marking and returning the ballot, and those responsible for counting the ballots. It should be remembered that, unless special provisions in the bylaws prevent it, a mail ballot may result in a decision based on a smaller percentage of participation than would be the case if the vote were taken in a regular meeting with a quorum present. One way to control this is for the bylaws to state that decisions by mail are valid only if a majority of a quorum of the members returns ballots.

Voting by mail is frequently used in elections, which may involve the use of a preferential ballot, but may be used for other purposes as well. Organizations may run out of time in their meetings and decide to determine a pending question by a mail ballot rather than by calling additional meetings. Only main motions, not procedural motions growing out of the consideration of main motions, should be voted on by mail.

It should not be possible to order a vote by mail on less than a majority vote. Otherwise, a minority may prevent a majority from taking legitimate action in a meeting. Once a decision has been reached on a motion by a majority vote, it should not be possible to nullify that decision by ordering a vote by mail. Of course, if it later becomes apparent that a mail vote is desirable, the earlier vote may be reconsidered and a mail vote ordered, if consistent with the bylaws.

A vote by mail is often used by large organizations and corporations whose memberships are widely scattered geographically. Officers are elected, proxies determined (see the next section), and propositions submitted for decisions on a ballot mailed to the members with instructions and, often, an envelope.

This cannot be said to be a "secret ballot," although it comes close to being secret if the marked ballot is sealed in an envelope that is signed by the voter and this envelope is mailed in a second envelope. The ballots themselves are not signed or identified in any way. The tellers compare the signatures on the envelopes against a signed membership roster to determine the legality of ballots submitted. There must be provisions made to verify the legality of votes, and this procedure does so while retaining a reasonable degree of secrecy. A variation is to have the ballots sent, in signed envelopes, to a post office box rented for this purpose and opened on a predetermined date and in the presence of neutral observers. Only one envelope is needed with this method.

Sometimes ballots are distributed in a meeting and, to save time, members are requested to mark, sign, and mail the ballots to the secretary, the chief teller, or someone else designated to receive them. This procedure, sometimes called *open signed ballots*, is no improvement in terms of secrecy upon the method just mentioned, since someone still must verify the authenticity of the ballots.

Brief statements of the positions for and against the motion to be voted on, or a summary of the qualifications of the candidates, may be mailed with the ballots to remind voters of pertinent information.

The Vote by Proxy

To vote *by proxy*, one member gives written authorization to another member to vote for him or her. Sometimes a member may vote several proxies; in corporations that allow one vote for each share of stock, a member may be authorized by others to vote hundreds of proxies. Unless specifically provided for in the bylaws of an organization, voting by proxy is not permitted; in the opinion of some, a deliberative assembly would be well advised not to allow it. The procedure conflicts with the basic principle of equality of membership.[1]

Preferential Voting

On a *preferential ballot*, voters mark not only their first choice but also their second, third, and so on, ranking their choices in decreasing order of preference.

Some organizations tend to shy away from any form of preferential voting, as if it involved some sort of trickery. This is unfortunate, because it can save substantial time in the election of officers. A principal advantage of preferential voting is to assure the completion of an election, or of the choice between propositions, with only one ballot. Many organizations could profit by looking into the various forms of preferential and proportional voting and, perhaps, including in their bylaws improved

---

1. Byrl A. Whitney, in "Proxy Voting," *Parliamentary Journal* 6 (January 1965): 8≈12, recommends that parliamentarians urge organizations not to legalize proxy voting by including provisions for it in their bylaws.

procedures for electing officers, members of standing committees, members of boards, and the like.[2]

Voting by preferential ballot is discussed in Chapter 10. When both the "hardware" and the "know-how" are available to an organization, a preferential ballot designed for processing by a computer will greatly simplify the operation.

---

2. For further information, see John H. Humphreys, *Proportional Representation* (London: Methuen & Company, Ltd., 1911); E. M. Bacon and Morrill Wyman, *Direct Elections and Law-Making by Popular Vote* (Boston: Houghton Mifflin, 1912); W. J. M. MacKenzie, *Free Elections* (New York: Holt Rinehart & Company, 1958); Robert W. English, *A Realistic View of the Hare System of Preferential Balloting*, 3rd ed. (Chicago: American Institute of Parliamentarians, 1964); and *Robert's Rules of Order Newly Revised*, 9th ed. (Glenview, Ill.: ScottForesman, 1990), pp. 418≈421.

Chapter 10

Nominations and Elections

Elections held by relatively small informal volunteer organizations need not be complicated. On the day of the announced election, the presiding officer asks for nominations from the floor for the office of, say, president. Perhaps one, two, or three candidates are nominated. When a pause indicates that no further nominations are forthcoming, the presiding officer announces that the nominations are closed, and instructs the tellers to distribute the ballots.

The presiding officer requests every member to indicate his or her choice by writing a nominee's name on the ballot, folding the ballot, and passing it to the aisle for collection by a teller. When all the ballots have been collected, including those of the presiding officer, the secretary, and the tellers, the ballots are canvassed by the tellers. *Canvassing* the ballots means more than just counting. It includes evaluating ballots to identify those that are invalid, blank, cast for illegal nominees, illegible, abstaining, and the like, and reporting the total results to the presiding officer for his announcement of the results.

If a nominee has received a majority of the votes cast, the presiding officer announces the winner of the election. Nominations are then in order for the next office, and the procedure is repeated until each office has been filled. In the majority of cases, there are no complications.

Since one must be ready, however, to deal with complicated situations that can arise in elections, this chapter will discuss in more detail the selection of nominees and some variations in the voting process. Organizations should include in their bylaws a description of all offices and the eligibility qualifications, duties, and terms of office for each. The bylaws should also include necessary instructions for conducting the elections of members to office.

Nominations

Theoretically, each member has the right to nominate the candidate of her or his choice for each office to be filled. But when members view objectively the qualifications and experience required for a particular office, and the likelihood of their nominee being elected, the field of eligible candidates is narrowed considerably. Furthermore, it often happens that experienced, qualified members cannot, in all fairness, permit their names to be offered in nomination because they have too little time or poor health, because their jobs take them out of town too often, or for other similar reasons. When all factors have been considered, there is usually rather a narrow field of nominees available.

From the Floor

When nominations are called for from the floor, a member may rise and state, "Mr. Chairperson, I nominate Joe Smith for treasurer." The presiding officer acknowledges the nomination, usually by saying, "Joe Smith has been nominated. Are there other nominations?" Nominations do not need a second, although seconding speeches are sometimes presented in support of a candidate. In small assemblies, members often make their nominations while remaining seated. The secretary records the nominations in the minutes. If only one candidate is nominated for an office, the presiding officer may, unless the rules require a vote by ballot, announce, "Since Mr. Smith is the only nominee for the office of treasurer, and a ballot vote is not required, I hereby declare him elected, if there is no objection."

When one or more candidates have been nominated and further nominations appear not to be forthcoming, the presiding officer should declare the nominations closed and proceed with the election. A motion To Close the Nominations (discussed in Chapter 6) is not necessary and even if passed could not prevent members from writing the names of the candidates of their choice on their ballots, whether or not they had been formally nominated.

If the number of nominees appears to be becoming cumbersome, the presiding officer may explain that too many nominees overly complicates the voting process and remind the members that other offices are also to be filled. Usually such a statement will prompt a few nominees, sensing that they have little chance of being elected, to withdraw their names. Too many nominees is seldom a problem; more frequently, the opposite occurs.

With several nominees remaining in the running, the balloting should proceed. If there is a large number of nominees, it may be agreed by a majority vote *before* the balloting that the two or three candidates receiving the least votes on the first ballot will be dropped, and if necessary the process repeated, until one nominee receives a majority vote. The use of preferential balloting, discussed later in this chapter, makes only one ballot necessary in such cases.

By Committee

In larger organizations, many of which meet only at the time of their annual convention, nominations from the floor are not considered practical. A *nominating committee* serves the important function of selecting nominees, and the bylaws of the organization may stipulate that nominations will not be received from the floor. The committee's members may be appointed or elected, according to the bylaws. It is preferable that the committee be elected, since this procedure prevents the president or presiding officer from appointing to the committee only those who will nominate candidates who favor continuing his or her policies. The committee must be large enough to be representative of various interest groups and geographic areas. Thus, a nominating committee with twelve or fifteen members, or more, is not unusual. If provided for in the bylaws, the member receiving the largest number of votes may be declared the presiding officer. If no such provision is made, the members may elect their own presiding officer.

Sometimes a nominating committee, in addition to making nominations for offices, nominates a list of members, perhaps two or three times the size of the committee, for election, usually by mail, to the next nominating committee. This procedure assures continuity. It is often stipulated that a member is not eligible to serve more than two terms in succession, or more than a total of a certain number of years, to prevent the committee from perpetuating itself.

The nominating committee may meet several times to draw up a slate of candidates for its report. Committees whose members are widely scattered geographically may circulate lists of names among the members by mail, or hold telephone conferences, to narrow the number of candidates. Normally, the committee must complete its report in time for inclusion in the program of the annual meeting or the meeting designated for the election. The committee should, of course, secure a member's agreement to serve if elected, before her or his name is included in the report of nominees.

Unless prohibited in the bylaws, nominations from the floor are requested by the presiding officer after the nominating committee has made its report, and nominees so selected are added to those nominated by the committee. No action is taken on the report of a nominating committee; the nominations it presents are treated as if they had been made by members from the floor.

The nominating committee may present only one

name for an office, or more, depending on instructions in the bylaws and on the committee's preferences. Organizations may require in their bylaws that the committee nominate at least two candidates for each office, but this is not frequently done. Candidates with little chance of election should not be nominated just to ensure the voters a choice.

By Petition

Some organizations provide for nominations by petition. In these cases, the bylaws instruct members that petitions bearing a specified number of signatures sponsoring a candidate will be accepted by a certain date prior to the election; usually, the organization supplies the appropriate forms to be used. Petitions judged to be in order result in the candidate's name being placed in nomination as if nominated from the floor. All details governing nomination by petition should be spelled out in the bylaws. A common error in formulating rules providing for nominating by petition is to require too many signatures.

Elections

Most organizations state in their bylaws that voting in elections will be conducted by secret ballot, or simply by ballot. A vote by ballot is usually taken to mean that voting is conducted so as to prevent disclosure of the members' votes. Voting by ballot should normally be used in all instances in which a member's vote, if disclosed, could be used to his or her disadvantage.

Voting

The most common ballot is a small piece of blank paper. The presiding officer requests that members vote by writing on the ballot the name of the candidate of their choice for the office in question. If the nominees' names are written on a blackboard and clearly numbered, the candidate's number may be used instead of a name. The usual procedure is to take separate votes for each office.

Alternatively, a ballot may be printed including the names of all nominees for all offices; the voter selects his or her choice for each office by marking an "X" in the appropriate space. A disadvantage of this method over balloting for each office separately is that losing nominees for major offices have no opportunity to be elected to lesser offices; that is, a losing nominee for president has lost the opportunity to be considered for vice president. The printed ballot is frequently used to elect officers of large organizations by mail. Enclosures outlining the qualifications of the candidates may be mailed with the ballots.

The presiding officer should conduct the election, not let it get out of hand. He or she should follow the procedure closely at each step. The presiding officer makes sure that each member has a ballot, and instructs the members to "Please mark your ballot" by using an agreed-upon procedure, then, after a slight pause, he or she requests that all ballots be folded and handed to the tellers. Before ballots are collected, the presiding officer makes sure that all members have voted who wish to vote, by inquiring, "Has each member present voted who wishes to vote?" If all have voted, he or she should announce, "The balloting is closed, and the tellers will please collect the ballots." Sometimes a brief recess is declared to await the results of canvassing the ballots.

The Use of Tellers

When voting by ballot has been planned in advance, such as for an election, the presiding officer should be ready to announce her or his selection of *tellers*, having probably secured their permission beforehand to serve. When a ballot vote has not been anticipated, the presiding officer will appoint tellers as needed. Usually, no less than three tellers are chosen, with the first named as chief teller. The chief teller divides the assembly into sections and assigns each teller to distribute and collect the ballots in his or her section. The chief teller also sees that the presiding officer and secretary, as well as the tellers themselves, are given ballots.

When all ballots appear to have been collected, the presiding officer inquires, "Have all the ballots been collected?" If so, she or he directs the tellers to retire to the place selected for canvassing. In votes, including elections, highly charged with emotional tension, the presiding officer may invite one or more members representing opposing points of view to observe the canvassing, with a firm understanding that they are only observers. In extreme cases, ballots may be canvassed in full view of the assembly.

When the ballots have been canvassed, the complete tally may be recorded as follows:

1.	Votes for	36
2.	Votes against	33
3.	Blank ballots	3
4.	Marked but invalid ballots	1
5.	Abstentions	2
6.	Total eligible valid votes cast	69
7.	Number required to pass (win)	36
8.	Result (Motion passed or lost; or _____ elected)	Passed

Marked but invalid (spoiled) ballots include those that cannot be deciphered and those cast for ineligible candidates. Also, two or more ballots folded together are counted as one illegal ballot. Errors in spelling do not make a ballot invalid if the intent of the voter is obvious. Blank ballots and those marked "abstaining" do not count in the total number of ballots cast as a basis for determining what constitutes a majority, although they may provide useful information toward determining the presence of a quorum. Invalid ballots do count in the total vote cast for determining a majority.

Announcing the Results

The chief teller presents the report to the presiding officer, who, after making sure he or she understands the report, announces the results. The ballots should be sealed in an envelope and given to the secretary, who keeps them at least until after the next meeting of the organization in case either a question arises requiring a check on the vote count or the assembly orders a recanvassing of the ballots.

Use of the Preferential Ballot

Some organizations use ballots that permit the voters to indicate not only their first choice but also their second and third choices, and so forth. This method has the major advantage of providing for the election of several nominees by one ballot, making unnecessary repeated balloting. For example, several members may be elected to a board, or faculty members to at-large membership on a college senate, on one ballot. One disadvantage of this method is that it may take longer to count the votes.

The ballot that follows is a sample ballot for preferential voting, adaptable for use by organizations.

If, at the end of the balloting, any nominee has a majority of first-choice votes in the total number of eligible votes cast, he or she is declared elected. If no nominee has a majority, the preferential ballot makes possible the use of second- and third-choice preferences to determine winning candidates. There are two ways to handle the ballots at this point; most tellers start by arranging the ballots in separate piles, according to first-choice votes for nominees.

Under the English system, sometimes called a Single Transferrable Vote System, the nominee who has the smallest number of first choices is dropped, and each ballot in that pile is "transferred" to that of the nominee ranked second. If the second choice on any ballot is a nominee already declared elected, the third choice on the ballot is "transferred" to the pile of the third-choice nominee. If, as a result of this transfer, any nominee receives a majority, he or she is declared elected. If there are only three nominees, and a tie results between the remaining two after dropping the third, the tie is decided in favor of the nominee who has the most original first choices. When there are more than three nominees, and

Preferential Ballot

Instructions: Vote for not more than 4 nominees. Mark your preferences by using 1, 2, 3, 4, with 1 representing your first choice, etc. Do not give any "tie" rankings.

FOR PRESIDENT

NOMINEES	RANK
Anna Chang	
Sarah Tackett	
Freeman Cousins	4
Marta Alvarez	1
Mary Lowe	3
Oliver Johnson	2
John Lawson	

when no winner is determined after the first transfer, the process is repeated. The transferred votes are added to the original totals, and the remaining nominee with the least number of first-choice votes is dropped; his or her ballots are transferred in the manner described above. The process is repeated until the required number of nominees receive majority votes, or until the number of "ballot piles" is reduced to the number of nominees to be elected. This method gives considerable weight to first-choice selections and, of course, prevents a nominee from winning who might, theoretically, have received all the second-choice votes.

Under what is called the American system, the nominee having the least number of first choices is dropped, but her or his ballots are not made use of in any way. Instead, the second-choice votes received by the remaining nominees are added to the first choices received by each, and a nominee is declared elected if the total of his or her first and second choices constitute a majority. If the new total is still short of a majority, the elimination process is repeated. The ballots of the nominee having the least number of combined first and second choices are eliminated, and the third choices received by the remaining nominees are added to the first and second choices each has received; the nominee who now has the highest number of first, second, and third choices is declared elected, assuming he or she has a majority of the eligible votes cast. A tie between two or more nominees is usually resolved in the same manner as under the English system.

Another plan, sometimes called the West Australian Plan, or the Hare≈Ware system, is an outgrowth of the electoral reforms advanced by Sir Thomas Hare in England in 1857. In this system, if only one nominee is to be elected, the first-choice ballots are counted and, if no one receives a majority, all but the two leading nominees are dropped. The ballots cast for defeated nominees are divided between the two remaining nominees in accordance with the preferences indicated on these ballots. Advocates of the West Australian Plan believe it the simplest in operation and the best method to reflect the will of the majority.

Still another method is the "low total" plan. This involves adding the "choices" cast for each nominee...that is, 1 for first choice, 2 for second choice, and so on...and declaring the nominees with the lowest total votes to be the winners. A random number, usually the number following the total number of nominees being elected, should be assigned to all unranked nominees on each ballot to assure that the total number of votes being added in each case is the same.

Voting by preferential ballot is not as desirable as direct voting by secret ballot in an organizational meeting. But when several nominees are to be elected at the same time, the preferential ballot saves valuable time for the assembly by delegating the job of counting to a few tellers. Prior agreement on the method of counting the preferential ballots is essential, since the various methods may not give identical results. And if nominees are to be elected by a plurality vote, authorization must be granted under the bylaws. A request that voters rank only the number of nominees to be elected will help the tellers. Members should be told that to give the same rankings to two or more nominees may invalidate their ballots.

Organizations interested in using preferential ballots should appoint members to study the various methods available and devise a ballot form suitable for their use.

Chapter 11

Constitutions, Bylaws, and Rules

Constitutions and Bylaws

Organizations traditionally have a constitution and a set of bylaws.[1] Very few have separate rules of order and standing rules. Organizations vary considerably in the degree of formality they use to state their basic rules and objectives. Each organization will need to decide for itself what form best suits its needs. A volunteer organization with a minimum of business to conduct in its meetings may get along well with only an undetailed set of bylaws articulating its name, purpose, committee structure, officers, and the like. A constitution may be eliminated entirely if the bylaws are rewritten to contain the information that formerly appeared in the constitution. For complex organizations, it is probably preferable to state rules of order and standing rules separately and to incorporate other data in a set of bylaws, omitting a constitution. Most groups find bylaws alone satisfactory.

---

1. A more complete and technical discussion of this subject may be found in Sturgis, *The Standard Code of Parliamentary Procedure*, 3rd ed. (New York: McGraw-Hill, 1988), pp. 193≈202.

Sample Bylaws, Standing Rules, and
Rules of Order
(Name of Organization)

BYLAWS
1. Name
2. Objectives and functions
3. Membership
   A. Qualifications
   B. Classes
   C. Dues
4. Officers
   A. Number and titles
   B. Selection procedure
   C. Duties and terms of office
5. Board of directors or executive committee
   A. Membership qualifications and number on board
   B. Duties and terms of Office
   C. Selection procedure including that for presiding officer
6. Meetings
   A. Regularly scheduled meetings
   B. Provision for special meetings
   C. Conditions governing advance notice to members of meetings and of agenda items requiring prior notice
   D. Rules for the protection of absentee members
7. Committees
   A. Standing committees
      (1) Membership
      (2) Selection procedure
      (3) Duties and terms of office
      (4) Selection procedure for presiding officer
   B. Provision for special committees
      (1) Selection procedure
      (2) Selection procedure for presiding officer
   C. Committee reports
8. Elections
   A. Nominating procedures
   B. Time and method of elections, including use of preferential balloting if desired

C. Votes required to elect

D. Provision for election without ballot of unopposed nominees

9. Quorum

    A. For assembly meetings

    B. For committees

10. Organizational discipline

    A. Nonpayment or late payment of dues

    B. For disciplining of members for other reasons

    C. Procedure for bringing charges, conducting hearings, impeaching, or suspending members

    D. Reinstatement procedures

11. Adoption of parliamentary authority

    A. Provision for adopting and for changing selection of parliamentary authority

    B. Application of authority with respect to adopted rules of order

12. Procedure for amending bylaws

STANDING RULES

1. Time for meetings to begin

2. Location of meetings

3. Policy on guests at meetings

4. Policy on special meetings closed to guests

5. Guest speakers

6. Responsibility for refreshments

7. Responsibility for lighting, noise control, public address system, heating, and the like

8. Procedure for amending standing rules

RULES OF ORDER

1. The order of business

2. Special rules governing length of speeches

3. Methods of voting, including authorization for mail ballots and preferential ballots

4. Conditions under which a plurality vote is acceptable in place of a majority vote

5. Procedural rules that differ from those in the parliamentary authority

6. Procedure for amending rules of order

A constitution usually consists of various "articles," designated by Roman numerals, each made up of many "sections" and "paragraphs" covering the subject matter of the article. A constitution always includes a procedure by which the constitution may be amended, stipulating how much advance notice is required of intention to amend, and how large a vote is required to adopt proposed amendments. Bylaws contain more specific information outlining the implementation of general policies stated in the constitution. Rules of order generally include procedural rules that vary from those stated in the adopted parliamentary authority. Standing rules deal with relatively minor points of organizational operation and require only a majority vote to change, while amendment of the bylaws and rules of order often requires previous notice of intent and a two-thirds vote.

Whether or not an organization has all four types of rules...a constitution, bylaws, rules of order, and standing rules...the essential information includes the official name and purpose of the organization and details regarding membership, officers and their duties, terms of office, election procedures, standing committees, provisions for meetings, the quorum, the adopted parliamentary authority, and requirements for adoption of amendments.

Many organizations would profit from a thorough study and revision of their constitutions and bylaws. Since constitutions and bylaws are adequately treated elsewhere,[2] this discussion will be limited to some general topics.

The adoption of an original constitution and/or set of bylaws requires only a majority vote. After adoption, the rules for amending will be those stated in the constitution and bylaws. The recommendation of a committee on bylaws (the term "bylaws" will be used to refer to both

---

2. Model constitutions, bylaws, and rules are available in the books listed in the bibliography by Davidson, Demeter, O'Brien, and Sturgis. Davidson includes, in addition, a checklist of eighteen "booby traps" (pp. 200≈202) against which a new constitution or set of bylaws may be checked for errors or omissions.

constitution and bylaws) is considered in the same way as is any motion embodying a committee recommendation, and is subject to the same amendments, referrals, and postponements as any other main motion. The appropriate motion from the committee is not, "I move the adoption of the committee report," but "I move that the following bylaws be adopted. . . ." Motions to amend the bylaws are main motions, although the terminology may become confusing as we speak of a main motion as an "amendment" to the bylaws.

Amendments to bylaws may be proposed by any member in good standing. Unless a procedure is developed to handle such requests, however, difficult situations may arise in meetings in which several individuals propose to amend the bylaws immediately, *if possible under the bylaws*, or announce their intention to propose amendments at the next meeting, if notice of intent is required at a prior meeting. Proposed amendments must be carefully considered to insure that they are consistent with existing policy as stated in the bylaws. Also, the language of a proposed amendment ought to be in keeping with that generally used in the bylaws.

A procedure adopted by some organizations to handle this situation appears to work well. A standing committee, possibly one on bylaw revision or on organization and rules, is charged with accepting proposed amendments, evaluating their merits, rewording them when necessary, and proposing them as main motions with committee recommendations for action by the assembly. This procedure is not meant to prevent members from proposing amendments, but to give their proposals a better chance for favorable consideration and adoption.

Sometimes organizations make it very difficult to amend their bylaws by requiring too large a number of members to vote for the change in order to pass it. This seems to arise from reluctance to change bylaws that have been labored over and extensively discussed in meetings and hearings. But often the changes are needed only a brief time after adopting the bylaws. It is a question of what constitutes responsible action by an assembly; leeway for correction of error should be ample.

Therefore, most organizations should probably permit amendment of the bylaws by no more than a two-thirds vote, or a majority vote provided previous notice has been given. The requirements of some organizations that the bylaws be amended by a two-thirds vote of the membership following previous notice, or a two-thirds vote of members present following previous notice, are difficult to fulfill...perhaps too difficult.

Organizations should include in their bylaws authorization for the presiding officer to declare an unopposed nominee elected without a ballot, if no one objects. This eliminates the awkward and undemocratic alternative of the secretary casting a ballot for the assembly declaring a nominee, if unopposed, elected. If a single member objects, of course, a ballot should be required; members should be privileged to submit blank ballots, or ballots bearing the name of any eligible candidate as well as that of the single announced nominee. The recommended procedure is not a unanimous vote but a vote without objection...if such is the case.

Most authorities agree that bylaws may not be suspended. But confusion sometimes arises when an organization wishes temporarily to suspend a rule of order or a standing rule, and the rule in question is found to be included in the bylaws. The problem here is not the one of legality, but of recognition that the rule should have been separately listed under an appropriate heading. The principle that bylaws may not be suspended is sound. However, a rule of order that has been incorporated into a bylaw may be suspended.

Standing Rules

Standing rules cover nonprocedural subjects. They may not be stated in the adopted parliamentary authority but are considered desirable to operate effectively. They are usually of minor importance by comparison with rules of order, and may therefore be authorized, deleted, or suspended by majority vote, unless an organization wishes to require otherwise. Some examples of standing rules are the following:

1. All scheduled meetings shall begin promptly at eight o'clock P.M.

2. Unless members are notified to the contrary, all meetings will be held in Brown Auditorium.

3. Guest speakers may receive honoraria of more than one hundred dollars only if approved in advance by the executive committee.

4. Any member who misses three meetings in succession, without providing a suitable excuse to the secretary, is subject to a fine not to exceed ten dollars.

5. Members may bring guests to all meetings except those described in the bylaws as closed meetings.

Rules of Order

Rules of order are those rules that govern the conduct of business by an organization: its parliamentary procedure. The parliamentary authority adopted as a procedural guide should be stipulated in the bylaws, since it should not be possible to suspend the parliamentary authority by suspending the rules, but only by amending the bylaw adopting it.

Any rule of order may be suspended (see To Suspend the Rules in Chapter 5), including rules stated in the adopted parliamentary authority, as long as this is limited to procedural rules controlling the conduct of business. However, the following rules, which are not rules of order, may not be suspended:

1. Conditions that govern the notice required to call a meeting

2. Quorum specifications

3. Specific voting methods, such as a requirement of secret ballots in elections

4. The vote required for particular purposes or motions

5. Provisions that protect absentee members

6. Provisions that prevent suspending a bylaw

7. Any provision that, if suspended, would deprive members of their basic rights

Under rules of order should be listed all those special procedural rules adopted by an organization that differ from those stated in the adopted parliamentary authority; these rules, which, of course, take priority over those in the adopted authority, may include the following:

1. The adopted order of business

2. Special rules governing the length of speeches

3. Methods of voting

4. Votes required to elect officers and committee members, if different from those specified in the adopted parliamentary authority

Normally, a two-thirds vote is required to suspend temporarily a rule of order, or to amend it, unless an assembly wishes to provide in its bylaws that a majority vote is sufficient following prior notice of intent to amend.

Annotated
Bibliography

Books

American Institute of Parliamentarians Staff. *Fundamentals of Parliamentary Law and Procedure.* 2nd ed. Dubuque, IA: Kendall/Hunt, 1992. 464 pp.

American Institute of Parliamentarians Staff. *Parliamentary Opinions Two.* Dubuque, IA: Kendall/Hunt, 1992. 176 pp.

American Institute of Parliamentarians Staff. *Readings in Parliamentary Law.* Dubuque, IA: Kendall/Hunt, 1992. 272 pp.

American Society of Legislative Clerks and Secretaries Staff. *Mason's Manual of Legislative Procedure.* Rev. ed. National Conference of State Legislatures, 1989. 677 pp. Written especially to meet the needs of "legislative and administrative bodies." The rules discussed are taken from judicial decisions and legislative precedents. Not intended as a parliamentary guide for voluntary organizations. Footnotes carry references to the many court decisions cited in the text.

Auer, J. Jeffery. *Essentials of Parliamentary Procedure.* 3rd ed. Englewood Cliffs, NJ: Prentice-Hall, 1959. 57 pp. A brief, clear restatement of *Robert's Rules.* Organizes motions by purpose: To Suppress Debate, To Delay Action, To Prevent Action, and the like.

Cushing, Luther S. *Manual of Parliamentary Practice: Rules for Proceeding and Debate in Deliberative Assemblies.* Revised and amplified by Paul E. Lowe. Philadelphia: David McKay, Co. 1925. 318 pp. See remarks on pages 15-16 in this book.

Davidson, Henry A. *Handbook of Parliamentary Procedure.* New York: Ronald Press, 1968. 300 pp. Largely a restatement of *Robert's Rules,* except for the abandonment of The Previous Question. Includes interesting chapters on "How Not to Get Pushed Around," "How to Handle a Heckler," and "Warehouse of Forms and Documents."

Demeter, George. *Demeter's Manual of Parliamentary Law and Procedure*: The Blue Book Edition. Boston: Little, Brown, & Co., 1969. 374 pp. A "revised, expanded, and updated" version of the book by the same title privately published in 1948 and revised several times before the 1969 edition. A restatement of *Robert's Rules,* it is very detailed and perhaps overly organized and lengthy. Includes many examples from the author's experiences in parliamentary practice. In Chapter 15, decisions from "500 court cases" are woven into statements of principles that will "help minimize, or avoid altogether, costly law suits."

English, Robert W. *A Realistic View of the Hare System of Preferential Balloting.* 3rd ed. Chicago: American Institute of Parliamentarians, 1964. 24 pp. Available from American Institute of Parliamentarians, 203 West Wayne Street, Suite 312, Ft. Wayne, IN 46802. Advantages and disadvantages of the Hare System, illustrations of its use, and detailed rules for canvassing ballots marked under the Hare system. Sample ballots included.

Hellman, Hugo. *Parliamentary Procedure.* New York: Macmillan, 1966. 113 pp. This textbook presents twenty-seven "lessons" organized around three major divisions: Participating as a Member, Presiding as Chairman, and Broadening Your Knowledge. Its "functional and practical approach" provides class exercises for practice and illustrative dialogues. An admirable attempt to simplify *Robert's Rules* is found in his discussion of "The Core Procedure" and "Special Emergency Procedures," and in his liberalization of the traditional precedence of motions.

Jefferson, Thomas. *A Manual of Parliamentary Practice: For the Use of the Senate of the United States*. Bedford, MA: Applewood Books, 1993. See remarks on page 15 in this book.

O'Brien, Joseph F. *Parliamentary Law for the Layman*. New York: Harper & Bros., 1952. 248 pp. A down-to-earth, commonsense approach, pleading for no more formal use of *Robert's Rules* than necessary. Advocates adapting formality of procedure to the degree of unity or division within a group on the question under consideration, and to the size of the group and its knowledge of parliamentary procedure. Written in a clear informal style.

Robert, Sarah Corbin et al. *Robert's Rules of Order Newly Revised*. Glenview, Ill.: ScottForesman, 1990. 706 pp. The ninth edition of this widely adopted parliamentary authority. See remarks on page 16 in this book.

Schlotzhauer, Virginia H., William J. Evans, and John R. Stipp. *Parliamentary Opinions: A Compilation and Revision of Opinions of the Opinions Committee, American Institute of Parliamentarians, 1958 to 1982*. Ft. Wayne, IN: American Institute of Parliamentarians, 1982. 199 pp.

Sturgis, Alice. *The Standard Code of Parliamentary Procedure*. 3rd ed. New York: McGraw-Hill, 1988. 275 pp. One of the best and most comprehensive works. Clarifies and adds to *Robert's Rules* and differs from it in minor ways, such as substituting "Vote Immediately" and "Postpone Temporarily" for the confusing "Previous Question" and "Lay on the Table" motions. Emphasizes conformity of procedure with court decisions, and has special chapters on parliamentary procedure for labor organizations, conventions, finances, staff, and consultants. The third edition includes two new chapters: one on handling discontinued motions and one on often-asked questions. This latter chapter (Chapter 30) is intended especially to aid persons unfamiliar with parliamentary procedure.

Periodicals

The following periodicals print many articles of interest to the student of parliamentary procedure, some of which are listed below.

Parliamentary Journal. Published in January, April, July, and October by The American Institute of Parliamentarians. March 1960-. Regularly includes articles of interest, including reviews, reports of research, and informal expressions of opinions by scholars and authorities on parliamentary procedure.

The Quarterly Journal of Speech. Published in February, April, October, and December by the Speech Communication Association. 1915-. (Under present title since February 1928; from 1915 to 1918, *The Quarterly Journal of Public Speaking*; from 1918 to 1928, *The Quarterly Journal of Speech Education.*)

G. W. Gray. "A Philosophy of Parliamentary Law" 27 (October 1941): 437-441.

J. F. O'Brien. "Henry M. Robert as Presiding Officer" 42 (April 1956): 157-162.

Communication Monographs (*Speech Monographs* until vol. 42). Published in March, June, August, and November by the Speech Communication Association, formerly Speech Association of America. September 1934-.

Kirt E. Montgomery. "Thomas B. Reed's Theory and Practice of Congressional Debating" 17 (March 1950): 65-74.

G. W. Gray. "Thomas Jefferson's Interest in Parliamentary Practice" 27 (November 1960): 315-322.

Communication Quarterly (formerly *Today's Speech*). Published in February, April, September, and November by The Eastern Communication Association. 1953-.

Ray E. Keesey. "Don't Ask the Parliamentarian" 8 (November 1960): 15.

Milton J. Wiksell. "Teaching Parliamentary Procedure to Adults" 9 (February 1961): 15-16.

J. Calvin Callaghan. "Do Ask the Parliamentarian… Beforehand" 9 (February 1961): 21.

A special issue, 4 (November 1956), on "Parliamentary Procedure" includes the following articles: Alice Sturgis, "American Voluntary Associations: Our Informal Government," 7-9. Paul Mason, "The Legal Side of Parliamentary Procedure," 9-14. J. Walter Reeves, "Nominations and Elections in Voluntary Organizations," 15-16. J. F. O'Brien, "The Chairman and His Job," 19-20.

Index